GOD-A-TUDE

An Attitude Based on the Word of God
that Brings Success to Your Life

DR. KAROCKAS "DOC ROCK" WATKINS

CONTENTS

ACKNOWLEDGEMENTS

First, I would like to thank my Lord and Savior Jesus Christ for giving me the gifts, passion, and purpose in life. I'd also like to thank the many people who have helped me learn and live for a cause bigger than myself throughout the years.

Additionally, my special thanks to my editor and writing coach, Adam Colwell. I could not have done this without your help and encouragement to do this project.

An additional thanks to the leadership team of Emmanuel: The Connection Church. Also, special thanks to my spiritual mentor, the late Dr. Maurice K. Wright, who taught me to be a true leader. Thanks to Dr. Halton "Skip" Horton for your drive to be excellent at the highest level. Thanks to Dr. David Green Jr. You gave me the confidence to shoot for the moon.

I am grateful to my parents, George and Johnnie Franklin, Curtis and Evetta Jackson, and in-laws, Noah and Hazel Boyett, for their love and support throughout the years. To my beautiful, lovely, committed wife, Audra, I appreciate what you do for our family and the sacrifices you have made. I am blessed to have three awesome children who love and encourage their father. Thank you Brianna, Christian, and Joshua!

ATTITUDE DETERMINES ALTITUDE

Everyone one of us has an attitude. Whether it's good, bad, or something in between, your attitude matters—but I have noticed that many people may not be aware of how their attitude plays a major part in their success in life.

As individuals, we were created in the image of God, so we should have a positive attitude that reflects that image. As I have examined my own attitude, success comes when it is governed by the power of God, but failure results when it is governed by the influences of this world.

Therefore, in order to reach our full potential, it is my prayer that people will develop what I call a "God-A-Tude" so their lives can begin to be productive and complete, enabled to achieve God's best for themselves and for others.

Simply put, a God-A-Tude is an attitude based on the Word of God that brings success in life. Yet many people suffer from bad attitudes. I know I did. For example, when I was an engineering student at Kettering University, recognized as one of the toughest engineering schools in the country, my mindset was that I was average, while other students had an attitude of high achievement, no matter the cost. My calculus teacher and mentor, Dr. David Green Jr., challenged me to believe that I could be one of the best.

This caused me to begin developing my God-A-Tude about dedication, grit, and success. A God-A-Tude of dedication means to never give up, no matter how hard it is or how bleak it looks, remaining committed to the end goal. A God-A-Tude of grit means to fight, to grind relentlessly with intensity and tenacity. Every morning, I had to have that attitude and walk in it, knowing that grit had to first occur in the mind before it could happen on the field. A God-A-Tude for success required fulfilling the mandate and calling on my life. It was not doing what everyone else was, but what I had been called to do, seeing it within myself and making it a reality.

Later, as a young engineer at International Business Machines Corporation (IBM), my attitude was again challenged by an IBM executive, Bob Dubose. He saw potential within me that my mindset had not yet recognized, and he wanted me to aspire to be at the top. I was doing good work, but he stretched me to think and do great work. To be stretched as a God-A-Tude means to open up our minds to believe that we can do more, realizing the excellence inside of us, and seeing ourselves able to advance to a different, higher position. Then, the God-A-Tude of great work is putting in the time, energy, and research, after we have stretched ourselves, to get to the desired end goal.

Our attitude is determined by the way we see and handle situations from a spiritual and mental perspective. Many, for example, view themselves from the stance of being a victim rather than a victor. I knew a gentleman who always saw himself as a failure. He'd blame others for what they thought about him and appropriate their thoughts as his own. I routinely talked to him about the power of mentally seeing himself as successful. I told him that if he could see his own success on the canvas of his imagination, he could have it. Doing this required forming a mental picture of where he could go, what he could be, or what he could have.

"You cannot have anything that you don't see," I said, "because it is a preview of a coming attraction and of what can possibly happen." I taught him that seeing his success allowed him to then form habits and disciplines to achieve that success. Today, that gentleman is doing well, running his own company that helps others get through life's crises.

Using the canvas of our imagination is an act of faith, and it is taken straight from Hebrews 11:1, which says "Faith is the certainty of things hoped for, a proof of things not seen." The Apostle Paul also told the Corinthian church that those who trust in God will triumph in all things through Jesus Christ. "Thanks be to God," it reads, "who always leads us in triumph in Christ, and through us reveals the fragrance of the knowledge of Him in every place." (2 Corinthians 2:14).

Others feel their attitude is expressed emotionally by getting sad or mad in certain situations, but our attitude is more than emotions and deeper than merely feeling down, angry, or frustrated. It's about how we see our lives, our goals, and our expectations when they are not being fulfilled. What we call depression or anger is really our attitude about our perceptions of what we have done or what we can do in the future. It's about whether we have control of those things, experience shortfalls, or are on target. The real issue is looking at what we have or have not accomplished in comparison to what we want to accomplish.

Once, I was very frustrated at where I was in my professional life. I felt that I had worked as hard as or harder than others, yet they seemed to be doing better than I was. I was playing a comparison game that I could not win. The more I looked at others, the angrier I got.

It wasn't until I changed my attitude about working, believing, and trusting God in my own grace, place, and space that I gained any peace. I had to look at myself, and what I was doing, thinking, and saying, to understand that I wasn't trying to achieve or become what someone else was. Instead, I needed a God-A-Tude that focused on doing my talents, gifts, and passions as He had called me to do them, and nothing more. I had to learn to be comfortable that the grace I'd received, the place I'd achieved, and the space I'd occupied was exactly where I was supposed to be, even if the grass seemed greener on the other side. My grace, place, and space were good for me and good for others. That allowed me to flourish.

If we are going to judge ourselves, our actions, or where we are at any given point, we do not need to compare ourselves to others. We judge according to what we know, who we know we are, and what we know we can do—and all of that is informed by what we know God has called us to do and be. No wonder Galatians 6:4-5 tells us, "Pay careful attention to your own work, for then you will get the satisfaction of a job well done, and you won't need to compare yourself to anyone else. For we are each responsible for our own conduct." (NLT) Theodore Roosevelt, our nation's twenty-sixth president, rightly and famously said, "Comparison is the thief of joy."

Throughout the Bible, God has given us tremendous insights on what our attitude should be. Paul encouraged the believers in Ephesus "to be renewed in the spirit of your minds." (Ephesians 4:23) He urged the Christians in Rome to "be transformed by the renewing of your mind." (Romans 12:2) Finally, Deuteronomy 28:13 says the Lord "will make you the head and not the tail, and you will only be above, and not be underneath, if you listen to the commandments of the Lord your God which I am commanding you today, to follow them carefully." Lots of people seemingly want to be first or the "head," to be on top, successful, and in control. But they'll never get there when they think like they're the "tail." Their mindset is on the bottom. Perhaps they don't want to work hard, failing to understand the many sacrifices that must happen in order to be the head. It could be that they accept failure as final, so that mindset keeps them thinking like someone on the bottom who is unsuccessful in fulfilling their goals, missions, and dreams in life.

I often say that many people bring their Bibles to church, their spouses to church, their problems to church, their shout, song, and dance to church, and even their money to church— but they don't bring their *minds* to church. In other words, they come expecting to be molded emotionally, but not to be challenged intellectually to the point where they change their mindset. They are not open to expect or to do something differently. They are willing to receive and get what they can out of the church experience, but they don't have the proper attitude that thinks about how they can take what they are hearing to move toward success or give back to others.

> **A God-A-Tude is a mentality that is put into action.**

A God-A-Tude is a mentality that is put into action.

In the end, your attitude is in direct proportion to your *altitude* in God. Swiss psychiatrist and balloonist Bertrand Piccard became the first person, along with colleague Brian

Jones, to complete a non-stop balloon flight around the globe. Piccard was quoted in National Geographic about the similarity he sees between balloon flight and daily life. "In the balloon, you are prisoners of the wind, and you go only in the direction of the wind," he said. "In life, people think they are prisoners of circumstance. But in the balloon, as in life, you can change altitude, and when you change altitude, you change direction. You are not a prisoner anymore."[1]

Our attitude changes our altitude and dictates our outlook. If I have an attitude that I won't be the best, that will drive me not to be promoted, go higher in my field, or create something new. I cannot go any higher than what I am thinking. On the flip side, if I am living in the projects, I can see myself going into my own home, driving a nice car, and doing things that others may not be able to do because my attitude will drive me to do whatever is necessary to achieve those goals. That's what I did. Even though I was in a situation that may not have been favorable, my attitude allowed me to change my altitude and rise out of that situation.

How we choose to think—our mindset—will not only affect what we expect from life and feel about God. It'll impact what we do in life and become for God.

I wrote *God-A-Tude* to encourage those who are pursuing the things of God and life with the proper attitude, and to transform those who have been struggling with having the proper and necessary attitude to succeed. After reading this book, I hope your mind will think and your mouth will say, "Bring it on, world! I can do all things through Christ who strengthens me!" (Philippians 4:13)

---

1 Richard Conniff, "Racing with the Wind," *National Geographic*, September 1997, p. 52-67.

1

GOD-A-TUDE DEFINED

An attitude based on the Word of God will bring success to your life.

You are where you are today based on the attitudes you had in the past, and who you will be in the future is based on the attitudes you have today. Better stated, you are today what you thought yesterday, and you will be tomorrow what you are thinking today.

Your attitude controls your success and failure—and it is time for it to give you more success.

Success, however, is not just the acquisition of material things or professional status. *Success is the accomplishment of an aim or purpose.* I discovered this to be true when I saw myself gaining some things that I never had but still being unfulfilled. It felt good in the moment, but there was no longevity to that feeling. As I asked myself, *What is this?*

I realized that fulfillment comes when we achieve or accomplish who we are called to be on this earth. I believe every person has the right to a successful life.

This requires you to discover your "why." It is the reason you exist, your purpose for living. Until you figure it out, you'll always think about the "how" and the "when," but never realize them.

Many times, our why is born from our gifts, talents, and struggles, and it is perhaps best seen as that one thing, if we had all the money in the world, that we would do for free. I tell people that their why is that thing that will get them out of the bed when everyone else is still hitting the snooze button. When we discover our why, we will search diligently to recognize how to accomplish it, and we will wait as long as it takes to gain the knowledge, stability, and experience to fulfill it. Then, the question of when our why happens is swallowed up in the journey of understanding it.

When I work with clients to help them discover their why, I ask them questions such as, "What is your passion?" "What is your educational background?" "What comes easy to you?" "What excites you?" I teach them that their why shouldn't be something that is done just for money, because when they find out what they are called to do, they'll never "work" a day in their lives. Living out their why will require work and lots of it, but it won't feel like work. Therefore, if they are complaining about what they do, are stressed out about it, or simply don't want to do it any longer, it wasn't their why to begin with. Their why, instead, will be based on their passion, and it will feed their commitment to it over the long haul.

When we know our why, it shifts us to a positive place— one where we can develop our God-A-Tude—because we know our purpose and have that thing in front of us that drives our emotions to be stable and to grow.

Times past

Growing up in the projects, government housing in a small town in Alabama, I didn't see many people who knew their why or had an attitude that reflected God's best for them and for others. What I did see were attitudes of religion, tradition, and mediocrity that were rooted in survival.

While I didn't formally accept Jesus Christ in front of people until I was 17 years old, I was a church kid, I knew God, and I accepted He was real. I loved church, and I loved going to church. Later as a boy, I'd travel with my stepfather, Dr. George Franklin, as he went and preached in country churches. Everyone from my family to my friends religiously went to church, but I didn't see anything that showed me they were really focusing on the Word of God after they left church. It was just something they did on Sunday, but after that, they went back to the same mindset of survival. They had the attitude that God was good, but they were not expecting that good in their lives.

I reasoned, *I don't want to be a part of that.*

At the same time, I saw many traditions that didn't seem to be helping anyone grow as people. These traditions seemed well and good on the surface: being nice to our neighbors, singing in the choir, or our church family helping one another. But they were done in a way that enabled the survival mindset rather than allowing people to move beyond it. It made me think of Christ's words in Matthew 7:6.

No, I thought, *I don't want to cast pearls to swine.*

With mediocrity, I saw people who were average. My definition of average is to be "on top of the bottom," and that's all everyone wanted. They didn't want to get all the way to the very top. I'd hear, "I'm gonna work, but I'm not going to go overboard," or, "I'm not going to extend myself in order to be my best."

But I don't want to be better than anyone else, I believed. *I want to be the best Karockas I can be.*

They settle. They're comfortable.

I want to be more.

I thank God for touching my heart and mind to see beyond what was shown to me so that I could envision His goodness and plan for my life. The Lord did this in a simple yet incredible way when I was just seven years old. Every summer, I stayed with my biological father's mother, Mama Sally, while my mother and stepfather spent more time with my two younger siblings, Brandon and Ashia. Mama Sally lived across town from where we did, only 15 minutes away, but her home was in the older projects while mine was in a government-assisted home that, while in slightly better condition, was still project housing. My biological father and I often went fishing during those summers, and Mama Sally usually joined us on those hot, summer mornings out on the Tennessee River.

My Mama Sally and I were very close. Even as a boy, I admired her hard work and entrepreneurship. She made Bee-Bops, Kool-Aid that is mixed and then frozen in cups, and sold them, along with pickled eggs, pickled bologna, homemade chocolate and vanilla cupcakes, and Little Debbie cakes to kids and adults in the neighborhood. I helped her shop during the week, and I assisted as she cleaned up the house, all of which brought us together.

As I did each evening, I was sitting at the table by the open window in her small, beige-painted kitchen, hoping to catch a breeze to cool the humidity that still pressed in even after the sun was setting. In the waning light, I could see the outline of the clotheslines against the darkening sky and the silhouette of the barrel grill in the small backyard. One particular night, I watched as Mama Sally made watermelon flavored Bee-Bops. She was very neat, so the only things out were what she needed at the moment: Kool-Aid, a jug, and a lot of white, pure cane sugar. It smelled so good! She often let me sample a spoonful to see if it was sweet enough.

Mama Sally put them in the freezer that covered one entire wall of the kitchen, and when she went into another room to do something else—God sent me an epiphany. It was as though the Lord Himself sat down across from me at the kitchen table to have a conversation.

"You have favor on your life. You are going to do great things to literally touch the world. Not just in Alabama, but in the world. So, trust me and walk in a place of discipline to get good grades and do what is right. Don't fear any other people of different races or in different cultures. One is no better than the other. They are all different, and I am going to use you in a special way."

> You have favor on your life. You are going to do great things to literally touch the world.

It was incredible and so real that I remember it today in such rich detail.

Prior to God revealing Himself to me that night, my attitude was that of a loser and a failure. I looked at my physical, social, and economic conditions as if they were what *I* was. Physically, I was smaller, slower, and uncoordinated compared to all the other boys who were good in sports. I was the cream puff, always the last person to get picked for the team. Socially, I was a little awkward. I liked reading, fishing, and being around older people and listening to them, so I was different than most of the guys around me. They were getting into trouble, and I wasn't. Economically, we lived in the projects. My mother and stepfather worked, but we just didn't have what most everybody else did. I thought we were not successful, and I knew I didn't want to live in subsidized housing when I was older.

Most people are products of their environment, but they can even be from a decent physical environment and still have no hope mentally or spiritually. Most of my aunts and uncles from my mother's side were on government assistance and codependent on one another. None of them graduated from high school. They had negative attitudes about life, education, and finances. Their mindset was, "I don't have anything, so don't ask me for anything. We are poor."

But when God spoke to me, He addressed my physical, social, and economic conditions with His words. He let me know that I was not a loser. I was not a failure. I had greatness within me. He gave me a vision that I would work with people of other races to achieve greatness.

At seven years of age, God gave me this magnificent word.

After God showed me His goodness and who I was in Him, my attitude began to change, and as it did, so did my life. I went from making failing scores in the first grade to being one of the top students in my elementary school. In fifth grade, Miss Pat O'Shield pushed me so that when I was in middle school, I wanted to be the best. My seventh-grade teacher, Miss Constantine Pope, pushed me even further. Neither one let me settle for being lowly. They had me thinking that I was the best and that I could achieve and *be* the best. That carried me successfully through high school, earning me a sponsorship with the General Motors Company to attend what was then the GMI Engineering and Management Institute (now Kettering University) in Flint, Michigan.

There, my attitude on life was challenged once again. It came in a most unexpected way from my college roommate, Michael Harris. He was making A's in his engineering classes while I was making B's. One morning at our apartment, I asked him to come to church with me. I was scheduled to preach the 11:00 a.m. Sunday morning message for the first time ever, and I was very excited about the opportunity. By the end of my sophomore year, I had felt God calling me to be a minister, and while in school, I started learning under Dr. Knox, the pastor of Ebenezer Baptist Church. Not only had I begun preaching, but I'd started a Bible study at the school on Thursday nights. Students of all races attended it.

So, I wanted to see if Michael would go to see me preach at Ebenezer. Always unapologetic, he was not at all hesitant to respond.

"You want to go preach and do all the Bible says you can do and all that," he said, "but you don't believe it yourself because I make A's and you make B's, and you are just as intelligent as I am. You don't have confidence in what you are preaching, so I'm not going to listen to you. Until your grades reflect what you are saying, I don't want to hear you."

Michael's candor made me mad—yet all the way to church, I was thinking, *He is right. I do believe God, but I don't believe the things I'm saying I can do through Him.*

As I calmed down, I began to consider what I needed to do to change. Not surprisingly, it began with my mindset. I had to start seeing things differently. I realized that I thought I had arrived when, in reality, I hadn't. *I've got to work on this. I can make A's. Why am I not making A's? What is stopping me from being my best?*

From that day onward, I began studying harder than I ever had before. I worked not only on my talents, but on refining them. I received the added encouragement I mentioned earlier from Dr. Green and applied it. Within a semester, the B's went to A's—and within that same semester, Michael saw what was going on, and he did go with me to church to hear me preach. Today, he watches me preach online just about every Sunday. He lives in Buffalo, New York, and he and his family visit me in Alabama every year.

I am grateful Michael boldly challenged me to change my mindset and take my attitude to the higher place of a God-A-Tude. I graduated with a mechanical engineering degree and earned honors on my thesis because of that God-A-Tude, and I now have a master's degree, two doctorates, and a certificate in business excellence. I own a leadership consulting company, I am chief executive officer of a leading nonprofit business, and I am on a team of cultural leadership consultants with a major insurance broker where I travel, teach, and train others around the world.

My why—to empower, lead, and teach people to reach their goals by helping them to maximize their potential—is being fulfilled.

Even better, so is the word that God gave me that hot, summer night at Mama Sally's house.

Attitude and philosophy

I believe millions of people fall short of living God's best for their lives because of a lack of excellence in their attitude or personal philosophy of success and growth.

Philosophy is derived from two words: *philo-,* meaning "to love," and *-osophy,* meaning "to think." So, our philosophy is simply "loving the way we think." That philosophy has been shaped by our history, the direct and indirect teachings we've received, our financial and social status, and other influences. Interestingly, the word "repent" has been believed to mean, "I'm sorry," but in the Bible, repent comes from the Greek word *meteneo,* which means "to turn our mindset for the better."

That is the product of attitude that informs our philosophy.

I derived the idea of a God-A-Tude from a revelation God gave to me that has its foundation in the Bible. Proverbs 3:5-6 directs, "Trust in the Lord with all your heart, And do not lean on your own understanding. In all your ways acknowledge Him, And He will make your paths straight." *All your ways* suggests that we are to trace our actions or reactions back to what the Bible speaks for that particular situation. We get in trouble when we base what we think or do on our present feelings. In addition, the devil and the world, and our flesh and self, will never want to exercise a God-A-Tude since the carnal mind "is enmity against God" and "to be carnally minded is death; but to be spiritually minded is life and peace." (Romans 8:6-7, KJV) Life and peace comes when we have a God-A-Tude where we are careful to check what we are saying, doing, and hearing in every area of our lives.

When God first spoke this revelation to me, He took me to Paul's writings to the church at Rome. "Do not be conformed to this world (this age), [fashioned after and adapted to its external, superficial customs], but be transformed (changed) by the [entire] renewal of your mind [by its new ideals and its new attitude], so that you may prove [for yourselves] what is the good and acceptable and perfect will of God, even the thing which is good and acceptable and perfect [in His sight for you]." (Romans 12:2, AMPC)

Clearly, Paul challenges us here to develop a new attitude based on the Word of God, not the world's superficial customs. Therefore, a God-A-Tude is a spiritual attitude that governs a person according to the ideals God has spoken for humanity. God wants us to live with a philosophy that is seen from His heavenly perspective, not the world's earthly viewpoint. After all, we are raised up and seated with Him "in the heavenly places in Christ Jesus." (Ephesians 2:6)

However, the sad reality is that many people struggle with having an attitude that informs their philosophy because they have not been renewed in the spirit of their mind, a term the Bible uses in Ephesians 4:21-23. "If indeed you have heard Him and have been taught in Him, just as truth is in Jesus, that, in reference to your former way of life, you are to rid yourselves of the old self, which is being corrupted in accordance with the lusts of deceit, and that you are to be renewed in the spirit of your minds."

Essential to this renewal is the determination within us to seek to please God and do His will or purposes in our lives. First Peter 4:1-2 teaches, "Therefore, since Christ has suffered in the flesh, arm yourselves also with the same purpose, because the one who has suffered in the flesh has ceased from sin, so as to live the rest of the time in the flesh no longer for human lusts, but for the will of God."

A greater understanding of this passage comes from its rendering in the Amplified Bible, Classic Edition: "So, since Christ suffered in the flesh for us, for you, arm yourselves with the same thought and purpose [patiently to suffer rather than fail to please God]. For whoever has suffered in the flesh [having the mind of Christ] is done with [intentional] sin [has stopped pleasing himself and the world, and pleases God], So that he can no longer spend the rest of his natural life living by [his] human appetites and desires, but [he lives] for what God wills."

Our attitude, then, is the spiritual mental agent that causes us to comprehend, see, and handle situations and circumstances in a certain way. It can be seen as the glasses through which we see the world. It controls the choices we make, the opportunities we pursue, the money we earn, and the success we achieve.

> Our attitude is the spiritual mental agent that causes us to comprehend, see, and handle situations.

Attitude even plays a significant role in how we read, pray, and perform. If we don't have the right attitude when we read, it is easy to criticize what we are reading, finding something wrong with every little thing that we consume. If we read with a positive attitude, though, we'll view it from a victor's standpoint. We'll find something, that one good nugget, that will help us go forward with our goals, dreams, and pursuits in life. When I first read *Emotional Intelligence 2.0*, coauthored by Travis Bradbury and Jean Greaves, I had a negative attitude about the notion that someone's emotional intelligence (EQ) was what made them successful as opposed to their IQ, or intelligence quotient. I thought good old-fashioned smarts was most important. But as I opened myself up and viewed the subject

11

of EQ through the lens of research, I quickly saw that EQ was both positive and beneficial. Not only did I go on to learn more about emotional intelligence, but I also became certified to facilitate EQ seminars, which I've now done around the world. Later, I have dedicated an entire section of this book to how EQ ties with having a God-A-Tude.

If we don't have the right attitude when we pray, we can be very judgmental on ourselves and others, all "woe is me" and venting in nature, and likely be praying for something that is not the will of God. Prayer cannot be done out of religious ritual, or just to see if we will get what we want, versus praying to have and deepen a relationship with God. Instead, prayer should be done with an attitude of seeking more of His presence: knowing who God is, what we can have, and what is in store for us in the future. That's when our prayers become more dynamic and effectual (James 5:16) as we start to see our prayers coming to fruition.

In 1996, my wife, Audra, and I started what is today Emmanuel The Connection Church in Huntsville, Alabama. Back then it was located in Decatur, Alabama, and the building burned down. The fire was confirmed to be a hate crime, and it was devastating. We had only been a ministry for a few months and had already done a lot of outreach in the community when it happened. After the tragedy, our natural inclination was to be fearful, hurt, and angry—but I knew we had to pray for a positive future and believe God had a greater plan for us. We focused on Romans 8:28 in our prayer meetings, trusting that God would work everything together for the good of those who loved Him, and we maintained that focus.

While the perpetrator of the hate crime was never identified, we became one of the first churches to receive a federal government loan so we could recover. The incident made national headlines, and I even got to go to Washington, D.C. where I represented our congregation and met with then-Vice President Al Gore, United States Attorney General Janet Reno, and Andrew Cuomo, who was serving as national director of housing and urban development. We experienced God's manifested favor and obtained a new building. To date, the National Coalition for Burned Churches and Community Empowerment has raised more than $50 million to rebuild 276 burned churches across the country.

Many people have gifts, degrees, and skills, but the reason they don't achieve their life goals is because they don't have a positive mental attitude about things such as their self-image. Years ago, there was a company that received a less than acceptable grade in their annual certification audit. The organization had talented individuals and a good management staff, but they were focused more on their skill sets than their mindsets. Top leadership challenged everyone to go from "good to great," using the book of the same name by Jim Collins. Changes were implemented in operations, policies and procedures, and overall work culture. As a result, the staff's mindset was elevated, and they became a unified team that was more productive and efficient. The next audit confirmed a 100-percent improvement in all facets of the company.

Contrary to what many people may assume, attitude is not always vocal or loud. It can be quiet but have loud results. I was involved in a situation with a city Chamber of Commerce where it wanted to take on a greater role when it came to diversity and equity in the community's culture. A lot of chamber members were opinionated about what we should do, how we should do it, and who should do it. But my attitude was to assess what was going on, view what we needed to do from the standpoint of the chamber's overall mission, and determine how I could help achieve that. As a result, without being the loudest person in the room, I became the chairman of the diversity, equity, and inclusion task force, and some very positive things have resulted from that role.

There was another occasion when a company wanted to do something internally to address racial equality. I met with one of its leaders who told me it was hard for them to find people of color to work in their institution. I suggested they could create such opportunities on their own, and I helped them set up a program with the business school at Alabama A&M University. Through this program, the company would hire two students to intern with them and become a part of their company, and it has been successful.

So, attitude can be managed and manifested in a variety of ways—but in the end, it is the part of our mental capacity that controls how we think and look at things from a spiritual viewpoint.

Attitude and how our mind functions

In Scripture, the word "heart" is rendered in Hebrew as *lev, leb* or *levav*. It is interpreted as the center of human thought and spiritual life. We tend to look at the heart as being mainly the seat of our emotions, but in ancient cultures, the heart was the seat of intelligence. The mind and heart, therefore, are one in the sense of *thought*. No wonder Proverbs 23:7 says that as a man "thinks in his heart, so is he." (AMP)

Humans are tripartite in nature. Each one of us is composed of body, soul, and spirit (1 Thessalonians 5:23). Our bodies are from the earth and temporal. Our spirits are from

God and eternal. Our souls are the place in which our mind resides—and our mind can be broken up into three compartments: the conscious, the subconscious, and our conscience. All three are involved in transforming our mindset to change our attitude to a God-A-Tude. This change is the product of human effort sustained by divine help from God.

Let's look at each one.

- **The conscious mind** is where our purposeful thoughts, as well as our initial reasoning and logical thinking, take place.

- **The subconscious mind** is the autopilot of the conscious mind and has the responsibility to automatically carry out the finished work of the conscious mind. When our conscious mind has accepted certain norms and values as truth, it is then the subconscious mind that takes that thought and handles our decision-making so that the conscious mind is freed up to receive and process new data.

- **Our conscience** is our belief system containing ethical and moral principles that control or inhibit our actions or thoughts according to our sense of right or wrong. It is our conscience that must be changed before *we* can change, as spoken of in 2 Corinthians 5:17. "Therefore if anyone is in Christ, this person is a new creation; the old things passed away; behold, new things have come." In order for us to become the successful people that we can be, our conscience must be transformed. While this process is launched the moment we receive Jesus Christ as Lord, the change requires a disciplined process of applying new truths to our lives. These new truths are learned from the Bible, prayer, and our church experiences. They can also come from books such as this one, godly and credible authority figures, our life experiences, and seminars that are not contradictory to our beliefs.

To prepare our heart and mind to have a God-A-Tude, we must continually make three essential decisions, without which it is impossible to reflect the attitude of God in our lives.

1. We must die to self.

Mark 8:34-37 taught this concept, mandating us to lose sight of our own interests, forget them entirely, and place God's interests first. It used the cross of Christ as a metaphor. Jesus said, "If anyone wants to come after Me, he must deny himself, take up his cross, and follow Me. For whoever wants to save his life will lose it, but whoever loses his life for My sake and the gospel's will save it. For what does it benefit a person to gain the whole world, and forfeit his soul? For what could a person give in exchange for his soul?" Remember what resides in our soul? Our heart and mind.

If we don't die to self, we will always second-guess God and lean to our own understanding. Matthew 6:33 instructs us to seek God's Kingdom and His righteousness first. This positions us to deny our own selfish ambitions and take up God's desires for our lives. This doesn't mean we cannot have goals, but it does mean those goals must be aligned with what God wants for us, not just something we desire.

As a boy, I had always wanted to be a medical doctor. I would read my mom's nursing books, and I took all the science classes I could in high school. One day, while I was contemplating how to get into and pay for medical school, I visited a doctor. He was my mother's colleague, so I knew he would be a great person to give some good advice and serve as a sounding board for my goals.

His first question shocked me.

"What has God called you to do?"

He went on to explain that he became a doctor because God had called him to go into that field. Furthermore, he said his practice was successful because he was doing the will of God. He counseled me to let God lead me into my future goals, and if the medical field was where the Lord wanted me to be, he would help me get into a program to pay for my schooling. The doctor was aware of my grades and my capabilities, but he told me to return to him for help only after I had heard from God.

Let me tell you, I had to do some dying to self after that conversation. I knew what God had spoken to me earlier. He had told me He was going to use me to touch the world, and I already perceived He was calling me into Christian ministry.

I never made it back to that doctor— but God has richly blessed me spiritually and financially as I died to self and followed His will for my life.

> God has richly blessed me spiritually and financially as I died to self.

2. We must die to our flesh.

In Romans 8, Paul taught the Christians in Rome about their flesh. He told them, "Now the mind of the flesh [which is sense and reason without the Holy Spirit] is death [death that comprises all the miseries arising from sin, both here and hereafter]. But the mind of the [Holy] Spirit is life and [soul] peace [both now and forever]. [That is] because the mind of the flesh [with its carnal thoughts and purposes] is hostile to God, for it does not submit itself to God's Law; indeed it cannot." (Romans 8:6-7, AMPC)

In our reasoning and thought processes, we must rely on the Holy Spirit. Our flesh will naturally fight against what God tells us to do. It wages war against our God-A-Tude, causing it to grow weary and stagnant. I've heard many Christians use the excuse that they are "only human" when it comes to ungodly attitudes where their actions and reactions to life's situations are not based on biblical precepts.

Early in my professional career, there were times I wanted my name to be everywhere. I desired fame and fortune, and I wanted it right away. I didn't want to wait or work for it. I didn't want it for the glory of God or even to help people. I wanted it because it was what *I* wanted. My ego and selfish ambition were manifestations of my flesh—and they had to die. I had to commit to myself that fame wasn't important. My name didn't need to be everywhere. The name of Jesus had to be glorified, not mine.

As I killed my flesh, helping others became most important to me. That has allowed me to fulfill the words of the genius theoretical theorist Albert Einstein. "Try not to become a man of success, but rather try to become a man of value."

3. We must die to the world.

Paul taught us to not be conformed to this world (or this age) in Romans 12, but to develop a new attitude based on the Bible instead of the world's superficial customs. That starts by dying to the way the world sees success.

There was a time early in my career when I was trying to advance as a young engineer at General Motors. My attitude was simple: get there by any means necessary as long as I didn't do anything illegal. I picked up that mentality at Kettering, where we were taught to be cut-throat in everything we did. Therefore, I wasn't taking into account the feelings and needs of others, and I certainly wasn't a team player. I was in it for myself. That was how the world did things.

Then I was challenged by a seasoned Christian engineer about my goals and plans for the future. He told me I was not displaying the right attitude, and he taught me about being a servant leader: a person who can have goals and dreams, but who puts other people and his team first. He helped me to understand that what I wanted to achieve could only be done with the aid of my colleagues. As someone once said, "If you live your life as if everything is about you, you will be left with just that. Just you."

I didn't want that, and I took his advice. As I went to work on a new project, a specific machine for operations, I consulted with everybody on that line. I listened to their ideas and applied them. I asked, "What do you believe will make this work?" "How can I help you achieve that?" I made it about *them.*

When it was time to present the machine to the top brass from headquarters, I declared that we, the team, did it. We accomplished it together.

I got more accolades for that project than anything I had done up to that point. Why? Because I killed the world's view of how to be successful and became a servant leader. I adopted the biblical view of success by esteeming others greater than myself (Philippians 2:3).

Both an eagle and a chicken are classified as birds. They have wings, and each one can elevate off the surface of the earth. But we can distinguish that a certain bird is an eagle because an eagle flies high on mountain cliffs, will fly into the storm toward the sun, and demands respect as it searches for its prey. A chicken, on the other hand, only flies as high as the barnyard fence. It plucks with its head down toward the ground when looking for food. Its power is trivial compared to the eagle.

I like the chicken, but I thank God He gave us the wings of an eagle. I don't want to hang out with chickens. I eat chickens. I want to hang out with eagles because they soar high, and I want to fly like one.

That requires confidence—a God-A-Tude that we'll explore next.

2

GOD-A-TUDE OF CONFIDENCE

Be strong and courageous
in your thoughts and actions.

In Joshua 1, we meet the man who was second in command to Moses and chosen by God to lead the Israelite people into the Promised Land after Moses died. Considered to be a biblical role model for the servant leadership principle I mentioned in the previous chapter, Joshua aligned himself with a proper attitude for victory.

That meant he had to align himself with God.

Right after Moses passed away, the Lord spoke to Joshua. "Just as I have been with Moses, I will be with you; I will not desert you nor abandon you. Be strong and courageous, for you shall give this people possession of the land which I swore to their fathers to give them. Only be strong and very courageous; be careful to do according to all the Law which Moses My servant commanded you; do not turn from it to the right or to the left, so that you may achieve success wherever you go." (Joshua 1:5-7)

God told Joshua to take on the characteristics of strength and courage and to obey Him so that he would be prosperous and successful. Joshua did just that. He led the Israelites into the land God had set aside for them and became one of the Bible's greatest military leaders for directing the seven-year conquest of the Promised Land.

More than that, Joshua became a man who prioritized God in his life. He later declared to the people, "If it is disagreeable in your sight to serve the Lord, choose for yourselves today whom you will serve . . . but as for me and my house, we will serve the Lord." (Joshua 24:15)

To have a God-A-Tude of Confidence, we must develop our strength and courage to hold fast to what God has purposed for our lives. Many people have attitudes of fear and weakness because they do not renew their minds in the areas of boldness and power in God. Yet true confidence only comes from reliance on and obedience to the Lord.

When our church burned down years ago, it shocked our world and shook our confidence. We were scared, confused, and without any means to acquire a new place to have our services. It took courage to trust in God that all things would work for our good, and prayer became our escape and helped us to possess the strength of a lion to plow forward. We had to face our fears to advance.

As we prayed for God to give us wisdom and provision, we realized that even though we had been victimized by others, the Lord was going to help us *through* others. God became our source. Everything and everybody else were the resource. That gave us strength and courage.

Attitude is the father of behavior

No amount of training in leadership skills, courses in management methods, power titles, promotions, or associations can be a substitute for having the right attitude. Attitude is the power of visualized victory, and this mindset is a natural by-product of the integration of our self-worth, self-esteem, and sense of value or significance.

> **Attitude is the power of visualized victory.**

Scripture addresses self-worth in Jeremiah 29:11. "For I know the plans I have for you, declares the Lord, plans for welfare and not for evil, to give you a future and a hope." (ESV) This teaches us that we are to contribute to society with importance and meaning.

Self-esteem is affirmed in Psalm 139:13-14. Speaking of God, David wrote, "For you formed my inward parts; you knitted me together in my mother's womb. I praise you, for I am fearfully and wonderfully made. Wonderful are your works; my soul knows it very well." (ESV) We should think and feel good about ourselves. We were created by God in a powerful and positive way.

Our sense of value or significance is declared in Genesis 1:28. "And God blessed them. And God said to them, 'Be fruitful and multiply and fill the earth and subdue it, and have dominion over the fish of the sea and over the birds of the heavens and over every living thing that moves on the earth.'" (ESV) We were made to conquer and to reign. Our attitude should be the attitude of a king. We must think to rule, not over individuals, but over situations.

In essence, our attitude is the manifestation of who we think we are, for good or for bad. Attitude dictates our responses to the present and determines the quality of our future. To put it more personally, you are your attitude, and your attitude is you. If you do not control your attitude, it will control you. It will propel you forward or knock you backward. Attitude is always the father of behavior—and when you allow God's truth to lead your mindset, confidence and success will follow.

Attitude also determines your success or failure in any venture in life. More opportunities have been lost, withheld, or forfeited because of a poor attitude than from anything else. More powerful than the pain of the past or the confusion of the present, the right attitude and the confidence it brings can turn darkness to light and make small become big.

Attitude directly impacts our decisions, the *quality* of our commitment to those decisions, and how well we *remain* committed to those decisions. Decision-making is a product of our attitude since our attitude helps to form opinions and ideas in daily living. When we are in the process of making a decision, our mindset will determine our choices.

There are seven attitudes that produce failure. Let's briefly look at each one.

1. **Arrogance** is defined as an attitude of superiority manifested in an overbearing manner or in presumptuous claims or assumptions. When we have an arrogant attitude, we fail to listen to constructive criticism and knowledge from others. Many times, this hinders us from making vital decisions that'll cause us to mature personally or help in the strategic growth of an organization.

2. **Judgmentalism** is an attitude that forms opinions about others that are usually harsh and critical in

nature. This leads to failure because it negatively affects solid relationships and alienates people. Such relationship bankruptcy leaves us without the support we need to grow and move to higher levels in our goals and career.

3. **Jealousy and envy** are connected to our inability to see what God has provided in our lives and causes a lack of thankfulness. James 3:16 states, "For where envy and self-seeking exist, confusion and every evil thing are there." (NKJV) While many believe that being jealous means fearing someone will take what we have while being envious means desiring what someone else has, historical usage shows that both mean to be covetous and are interchangeable when describing having a desire for someone else's possessions. So, when we possess this type of attitude, we are not open to engaging in genuine and serious team comradery that enables us and the group to be successful.

4. **Boastfulness** is an expression of excessive self-pride. This attitude causes us to not fully look at ourselves and keeps us from seeing the negative traits or behaviors that we need to improve to avoid failure.

5. **Comparison** is judging ourselves based on what others are thinking or doing. Events such as a promotion, a divorce, an empty nest, or retirement can cause us to inspect who we are in relation to someone else. This can leave us feeling insecure, anxious, or confused. This is not a healthy mindset and can lead to a slow decline of our self-esteem.

6. **Negative competition** is when we compete with others in such a way that we want to win by any means

necessary, even at the expense of others. This attitude shuts down the trust and psychological safety of a team, and negatively impacts the overall culture of an organization, eating away at teamwork and relationships.

7. **Disobedience** is an attitude where we refuse to obey rules or authority. This gives ground to undisciplined actions and leads to systemic failures. Disobedience is dangerous, in that we may feel like we are succeeding when, in reality, destruction is just down the road.

Conversely, there are seven attitudes that lead to success.

1. **Humility** is the quality of being humble and puts the needs of other people before our own as we think of others ahead of ourselves. This does not draw attention to us, and it can mean acknowledging that we are not always right. When we have this attitude, we allow others to achieve their best by not trying to upstage or grandstand anyone else.

2. **Teachableness** means we are ready to learn and open our hearts to new ideas, pursuits, and dreams. Having this attitude means we are willing to do whatever is necessary to gain knowledge on a particular subject, allowing us to stay on the top of our profession or ministry.

3. **Compassion** is an emotional response to sympathy and creates within us a desire to help others. It encourages us to see a need and not just give lip service to it, but actually take action toward solving it. It is an attitude that pulls people together to unite around a cause.

4. **Generosity** is the willingness to give of our time and our finances to benefit the recipient. Positive things happen when we give of ourselves. Author, salesperson, and motivational speaker, the late Zig Zigler, said, "You can have everything in life you want, if you will just help other people get what they want." An attitude of generosity causes us to be sacrificial, which aids in our maturity and leads to greater success in life.

5. **Diligence** is described by author Steven K. Scott in *The Richest Man Who Ever Lived: King Solomon's Secrets to Success, Wealth, and Happiness* as creative persistence, a smart-working effort rightly planned and performed in a timely, efficient, and effective manner to attain a pure and high-quality result. When we display this attitude, success is not an option for the future, but an obtainable outcome.

6. **Obedience** is compliance with an order, request, or law, or submission to another's authority. It carries with it a social influence connotation that causes others to comply to a certain direction of vision and thought. Obedience leads to discipline, enabling us to reach our goals and attain various levels of success.

7. **Focus** is the quality of having or producing a clear, visual definition. An attitude of focus lets us clearly see the vision ahead in the midst of many other distractions that try to take our eyes off of what is important. We go where our focus goes. Focus requires us to stay on top of our crafts and keep striving to be better.

Developing confidence from our attitude

An attitude of success breeds a God-A-Tude of Confidence to discover and live God's very best for our lives. Confidence is defined as an assurance, trust, or reliance on something or someone. In the case of the Christian, that confidence is in none other than Jesus Christ Himself.

When I first became chief executive officer at Ability Plus Inc. in Huntsville, the largest single provider of services for people with special needs in Alabama, it was failing financially. In addition, internal issues with staffing and leadership had taken their toll, and the people there had no confidence. I needed to trust in God alone to correct what was going on. He told me that He would never leave me nor forsake me, and I felt as though He had put me in that position at that particular time to do something different. Because of that conviction, I wasn't afraid of what would happen down the road, and when there were hard choices, we made them knowing that we would get back to a place higher than where we were before.

That was exactly what happened. I had an opportunity to influence leaders, teammates, and younger professionals by looking at our company's culture. In a year-and-a-half, we dramatically turned around that culture, and the company's bottom line, through teaching and mentorship. I worked with the staff to change their behavior and outlook on what was possible, and that instilled confidence. I encouraged people to do their best and then asked the question, "Are you sure that is your best?" As a result, they went above and beyond, didn't complain, and became innovative within their own departments, doing things in a smarter and more consistent way.

Personally, when our church burned down and I represented our congregation before leaders in the nation's capital, it was very intimidating. I had never been to Washington D.C. before, and I had never been in that kind of circle of influence. But I had confidence that God would see me through. The Lord reminded me that in the Bible, kings went to priests for advice. So, I told myself that I was the priest in this scenario, and they were the kings. Therefore, I should have confidence as the man of God, the one representing Christ and asking them for advice and help, knowing that God had my back.

Confidence in God does not come automatically with our salvation. Rather, confidence is an attribute that comes from our diligence in maintaining our relationship with the Lord and comes in direct proportion to the time we spend reading, studying, and applying God's Word. In 2 Timothy 2:15, Paul wrote, "Do your best to present yourself to God as one approved, a worker who has no need to be ashamed, rightly handling the word of truth." Every Christian who believes they have become the righteousness of God in Christ Jesus must have confidence that "he who began a good work in you will bring it to completion at the day of Jesus Christ." (Philippians 1:6).

Yet it is the devil's objective to keep us from putting our confidence in God, knowing that as we experience the Lord, we will have more faith in Him. As Romans 5:2-5 declares, "Through him we have also obtained access by faith into this grace in which we stand, and we rejoice in hope of the glory of God. Not only that, but we rejoice in our sufferings, knowing that suffering produces endurance, and endurance produces character, and character produces hope, and hope does not put us to shame, because God's love has been poured into our hearts through the Holy Spirit who has been given to us."

There are three ways people have confidence in God. The first two ways limit God's power to be manifested in their lives. The last brings blessing.

1. Desperation

Many have confidence in God through desperation, trusting Him only when they have exhausted all of their other resources. They have called on family, friends, and all others, and found no one who could help them. So, they turn to God last instead of first. That is not the correct way to have confidence in God. Remember, God is not a resource—He's the source. As Philippians 4:19 proclaims, "My God will supply every need of yours according to his riches in glory in Christ Jesus." Go to God first.

> Remember, God is not a resource— He's the source.

2. Deliberation

Others have confidence in God by deliberation. They will trust the Lord only as far as they can think out the process. If they have deliberated in their mind and see it working out within their own assessment, they will trust God to bring it to pass. But this is a carnal way of having confidence in God. The Lord tells us not to put our confidence in ourselves. We must be willing to trust God when everything in the natural tells us we can't, such as when Noah built the great ark in Genesis 6-8. It was illogical to believe it could rain enough for a flood to deluge the entire earth, but Noah didn't deliberate. He had confidence in the Lord and obeyed His command. Do the same. Seek and trust God's wisdom, then obey without question.

3. Revelation

Those with a God-A-Tude have confidence in God by revelation. As God reveals Himself through the Bible, they believe in Him and have total confidence in what He says. They are the ones who receive "the Spirit of wisdom and of revelation in the knowledge of him, having the eyes of your hearts enlightened, that you may know what is the hope to which he has called you, what are the riches of his glorious inheritance in the saints." (Ephesians 1:17-18) They do not trust in what they see in the natural, but they have a God-A-Tude of Confidence in God's supernatural power through His enlightened Word.

I once did a seminar at a large company. When I went to lunch with the CEO, he was impressed with my work in the area of leadership, and he asked if I would consider meeting with a few of his top leaders. I agreed, and we had the meeting, but a few months later I learned that one of the executives had a friend who did not care for me or my work. At first, I was very disappointed and felt like I had been attacked. But then the revelation of God's Word reminded me of the words from the prophet Isaiah, which says that "no weapon forged against you will succeed." (Isaiah 54:17) I took it to heart and changed my attitude about the situation. Six months later, that same company called me in to speak at their major annual event for all its employees. I met the executive whose friend did not like me, and he was cordial. The event was a success, and I was able to make a positive impact on that organization and its staff.

The Word of God also tells us to encourage one another (1 Thessalonians 5:11), and I allowed that principle to guide me as pastor of my church as I built strong relationships with community leaders. In the beginning, I didn't know them, and they didn't know me, but I needed them to do some things to help our outreach ministry. I figured that if I showed myself to be friendly and encouraged them, they would be open to receive what I had to say, and influential people would gravitate to some of the visions I had for the community—specifically, an afterschool program and a mentorship program to help youth find jobs.

One person was an especially influential guy in the city. We met because I was at the chamber of commerce, we became friends, and he pointed me to people who had block grants that we could apply for as a church. Thanks to his help, we were able to fund our program for kids where we taught them empowerment and leadership skills from 3:00-5:00 p.m. each weekday. We also provided food and clothing for those kids and others.

Signs of a lack of confidence

There are many signs that'll show up if we are not reflecting a God-A-Tude of Confidence. Each one is like a road signal that warns us that we are about to take a wrong turn, and each one will hurt our quest to live out God's best.

One sign is *frustration and anxiety*. Both indicate that we are upset about something that is not happening the way we thought it should. Yet we must constantly know and accept that God cannot fail and is in charge of our lives. Philippians 4:6-9 says it so well. "Do not be anxious about anything, but in everything by prayer and pleading with thanksgiving let your requests be made known to God. And the peace of God, which surpasses all comprehension, will guard your hearts and minds in Christ Jesus. Finally, brothers and sisters, whatever is true, whatever is honorable, whatever is right, whatever is pure, whatever is lovely, whatever is commendable, if there is any excellence and if anything worthy of praise, think about these things. As for the things you have learned and received and heard and seen in me, practice these things, and the God of peace will be with you."

Another sign that we are not reflecting a God-A-Tude of Confidence is *offensiveness*. Many times, offenses come up against us which are designed to knock down our confidence in God. They may be lack of acknowledgment, a correction to a certain negative behavior, or an absence of support. When we allow these offenses to get the best of us, we step out of the area of trusting in the Lord. We must not be shaken by what people say or how the enemy, Satan, tries to swallow our goals. Psalm 56:1-3 says, "Be merciful and gracious to me, O God, for man would trample me or devour me; all the day the adversary oppresses me. They that lie in wait for me would swallow me up or trample me all day long, for they are many who fight against me, O Most High! What time I am afraid, I will have confidence in and put my trust and reliance in You." (AMPC)

The next sign is *jealousy and envy*. There is no need to be jealous or envious of what someone has or something they have done. Remember, the Lord doesn't have big "I's" and little "You's." God is just and sovereign in all of His ways, and He doesn't regard one individual over another (Ephesians 6:9). Every person is important and plays his or her chosen role in what He wants to accomplish (1 Corinthians 12). No matter who you are or where you are from, there are opportunities for you to be a person of value and success.

The final sign that we are not reflecting a God-A-Tude of Confidence is *feeling down on ourselves*. This happens when we do not cast the entirety of our cares (all of our worries, concerns, and troubles) on the Lord, for He cares for us (1

Peter 5:7). We must totally trust God to work out, remove, and destroy the issues at the root of our feelings. We can live in victory and joy!

Having a *full* God-A-Tude of Confidence

It is dangerous to trust ourselves or anyone else without first having total confidence in God. Many times, people we've held as role models or mentors can have something unforeseen happen to them that causes us to lose our confidence because we placed our trust in the person, not in the God who works through that individual. Psalm 118:8-9 states, "It is better to trust in the Lord than to put confidence in man. It is better to trust in the Lord than to put confidence in princes." (KJV)

It is in Christ that we live, move, and have our being (Acts 17:28), so we must have a God-A-Tude that doesn't depend on others or ourselves, but on Him. Ministry leaders, for example, should never place their confidence in the people they serve or the amount of people in their congregation or on their donor rolls. Misplaced confidence in them may even cause these leaders to question the voice of God when He tells them to carry out a vision that the people can't see. In addition, many senior pastors, overseers, and bishops have hindered what God wants to do in their ministry because they have unduly placed their confidence in people, not God. My attitude as a pastor is to always trust God, and everything else will work out. My confidence is in Him, and Him alone.

> We must have a God-A-Tude that doesn't depend on others or ourselves, but on Him.

There are great rewards when we have a God-A-Tude of Confidence. We can rest assured that everything we put our hand to will prosper for Christ, and that He will complete it (Philippians 1:6). The devil never wants us to place our absolute confidence in God in this way. He will bring doubt, anxiety, fear, and low self-esteem to challenge our trust in Him. Yet Dr. I.V. Hilliard rightly said, "On the other side of your willingness to trust God as your source are some incredible life-changing experiences."

According to the book of Hebrews, our God-A-Tude of Confidence brings great reward. "Cast not away therefore your confidence, which hath great recompense of reward. For ye have need of patience, that, after ye have done the will of God, ye might receive the promise. For yet a little while, and he that shall come will come, and will not tarry." (Hebrews 10:35-37, KJV) Our confidence in God carries compensation. God blesses those who trust Him with their entire lives, and He wants us to experience the power of His trust. God can't go back on His promises! If the Lord said it, then we can have all the confidence in the world that He will bring it to pass—and we will see our goals and visions manifested.

3
GOD-A-TUDE
OF EMOTIONAL INTELLIGENCE

Give thought and self-reflection
to the emotional situations you encounter.

M any people get upset when pressures at work, frustrations at home, and other taxing life issues come upon them. When we don't have proper control over these situations, our attitude will reflect this through negative behavior.

According to Travis Bradberry, author of *Emotional Intelligence 2.0*, emotional intelligence is our ability to recognize and understand emotions in ourselves and others, and to use this awareness to manage our behavior and relationships. Daniel Goleman, regarded as the father of emotional intelligence, says EQ is managing feelings so that they are expressed appropriately and effectively, enabling people to work together smoothly toward their common goals. EQ expert Steve Hein defines emotional intelligence as the combination of innate emotional sensitivity with learned emotional management skills, which together lead to long-term happiness and survival.

When we first become aware of our own emotions and those of others, we can start to manage our attitude in such a way as to produce positive change and results. I see this discipline as being in line with the scriptural fruit of the Holy Spirit of self-control, also known as temperance (Galatians 5:23).

Therefore, to have self-control over our emotions, and the emotional reactions of others toward us, is a God-A-Tude of Emotional Intelligence.

Our attitude is a product of our behavior and is based on our self-esteem, self-image, and self-efficacy (how well we respond to potential situations). We must monitor our God-A-Tude of Emotional Intelligence daily to produce the positive mindset and behavior needed to get the desired results. It is very important that we continually work on managing what we feel and how our feelings affect others.

This is not something that just happens. We need to grow intentionally by placing our personal development on the forefront. We must give much thought and self-reflection to the emotional situations that we encounter every day. We can control our thoughts, and the attitudes that stem from them, when we understand them. I believe everyone wants to have the right attitude in times of peril, stress, and even triumph, but we often haven't developed the mindset to produce that attitude.

Emotional intelligence is commonly defined by five skills:

1. **Self-awareness** is the ability to recognize our own emotions and how they affect our thoughts and behavior. It also helps us to know our strengths and weaknesses, and to have self-confidence.

2. **Self-management** is the ability to understand changing situations and manage our feelings and behaviors in a healthy way. This produces a greater level of commitment and enables us to take on new and challenging things.

3. **Social awareness** is having empathy. This is the capacity to put ourselves in other people's shoes so we can feel their pain. We can do this by learning to understand their behavioral patterns, the differences in their personality types and temperaments, and being able to navigate through those differences.

4. **Relationship management** is the ability to influence other people to behave better and manage their own feelings. We do this by developing and maintaining good relationships, communicating clearly, inspiring others to work well in a team environment, and mediating conflict.

5. **Self-motivation** is a personal drive to improve and achieve, a commitment to goals and vision, and a desire to act on opportunities with optimism and resilience.

As we grow in these EQ skills, we will improve our attitude to produce a God-A-Tude of Emotional Intelligence. Let's take a closer, personal look at each one of these skills from that perspective.

Skill 1: Self-awareness

You must know yourself. That knowledge arms you to manage yourself effectively. If you are a stranger to your emotions, fears, or even your purpose, you will live a strange life, one not meant for you, and you will be helpless to the waves of emotions that will drive your actions and decisions wherever they please. This will result in you depending on other people to define you, and you will be ruled by their opinions of you.

Yet I believe the power to define is the power to determine destiny. In the Bible, 1 Timothy 4:16 says, "Pay close attention to yourself and to the teaching; persevere in these things, for as you do this you will save both yourself and those who hear you." As a CEO, I constantly do self-reflections to better understand my emotions in critical situations. I don't act without first running my reactions through a series of filters. I ask myself questions such as, "Is this beneficial to me or the process?" "What does it take to get it done?" "Is this the proper time?" The answers to these questions slow me down just enough to process my emotions and think through the decision I am about to make. They ensure that I am not permitting my opinions to sway me or allowing a vibe that has no legitimacy to persuade me. I am able to get past *me* and get to the issue at hand.

> I believe the power to define is the power to determine destiny.

Skill 2: Self-management

Self-management is the ability to train your mind to strengthen and increase in capacity so that it is empowered to accept your feelings and maximize its energy to exhibit the right behavior, attitude, actions, and words. Your mind is like a knife. If you sharpen it, it cuts faster. If you don't, it becomes dull and inefficient.

Your mind is one of the greatest gifts God gave you to help you live a successful life. But the imperfections associated with living dump a lot of junk into your mind. So, to get the best out of your mind, that junk has to be cleared out so your mind can be refurbished. A refurbished mind will help you maintain the right perception, and that's vital since you respond to issues based on what you perceive about them. For example, Proverbs 16:32 says, "One who is slow to anger is better than the mighty, And one who rules his spirit, than one who captures a city."

Through self-management, your mind is refurbished to allow its full potential to be reaped. Mind management takes care of personal and emotional management, and well managed emotions enable you to act, talk, and respond to issues in the right way, place, and time to the right people, as opposed to reacting to them. I'm quite intentional about managing my feelings and desires. There have been certain things that I felt like I needed right away, but I used the self-management strategy of delayed gratification to put them off for a more appropriate time. Delayed gratification is beneficial because it creates the time to build money, talent, or resources in order to obtain something. Then, when the opportune moment arrives, you'll have everything you need to be as productive and successful as possible.

I recall the time I had an opportunity to purchase another company. I really wanted it and would have bought it, but my self-management strategies helped me recognize that the purchase would've caused a major strain on the parent company. The company also had internal instability and some negative issues with client relations, so I decided it was best not to make the purchase. If I had not practiced delayed gratification, I may have jumped in with both feet and suffered severe consequences later.

Skill 3: Social awareness

Social awareness is a social skill that enables you to maintain harmony in your world through an existing inner peace. When you are able to understand other people's feelings and relate better to them, social awareness usually leads to positive action.

Result-oriented social awareness must be observant. You will need to study peoples' personality types to be able to understand their emotions. Through personality types, you will understand why others act, react, or talk a certain way. All three are the overflow of their emotional state. So, social awareness understands this and devises a means for you to manage them. This type of social awareness is described in Romans 12:15-16. "Rejoice with those who rejoice, and weep with those who weep. Be of the same mind toward one another; do not be haughty in mind, but associate with the lowly. Do not be wise in your own estimation."

I have learned how to put myself in other people's shoes and try to understand their point of view. Once, one of our Ability Plus house managers came to me. He oversaw staff and programs for several of the homes we serve. He told me, "We need more funding because our responsibility is to fulfill what the budget demands." So, I shadowed him for a few days to assess his concern and find out what his days were like. In doing so, I discovered that while there were some capacity issues, we actually didn't need to put more resources into the homes to address those needs. In fact, we pulled back on some things so that the house manager could improve his planning and overall leadership. Shadowing him also made me more empathetic to the concerns he was dealing with, which he appreciated. It was helpful to everyone.

Skill 4: Relationship management

Relationship management is the ability to influence other people to behave better and manage their own feelings. Having good social skills and interpersonal relationships is a major facet of managing other people. You will always have to relate with other people. Learning this skill is vital in order to relate well with others in the workplace, at home, or in any group.

People have different temperaments, likes, and dislikes, and they bring different kinds of energy and understanding to situations. These differences will play out in the way they act, respond, or talk—so if you can manage those differences, you can maintain peace and maximize the benefits of those relationships.

An example of proper relationship management is found in a Bible verse I mentioned in the previous chapter, 1 Thessalonians 5:11, which says, "Therefore encourage and comfort one another and build up one another, just as you are doing." (AMP) I often teach others about their value and worth both to themselves and to their organizations. One time, I brought all of our mid-level managers together to participate in teamwork exercises designed to enhance our concern for one another and help overall production. These exercises focused on what they would do if they were in their peer's position in the company. They asked questions like, "What decisions would you make?" "How would you act?" We had role play sessions to help everyone appreciate what each person was doing and how each one brought value to the company. It built better relationships among the management team.

Skill 5: Self-motivation

Self-motivation is the ability to stir yourself to do what needs to be done without influence from other people. Another word for self-motivation is self-encouragement. Self-motivated people are enthusiastic. They have the ability to complete a task even in the face of barriers.

A crucial part of self-motivation is decision making. This can be daunting, and it can pull strongly on your emotions. Making hard decisions is not always easy, and it can be damaging if not properly handled. Every decision has consequences, and your decisions today will determine your quality of life tomorrow. Your decisions sculpt your destiny.

> Your decisions sculpt your destiny.

The Apostle Paul wrote about his self-motivation and how it impacted his decision making in Philippians 4:12-13. "I know how to get along with little, and I also know how to live in prosperity; in any and every circumstance I have learned the secret of being filled and going hungry, both of having abundance and suffering need. I can do all things through Him who strengthens me."

One of the things I do to motivate myself is to tell myself there are *no* bad days. I started doing this years ago after my church had gone through a transition. I changed our philosophy from one of just religiosity to becoming a place of empowerment and learning. I invited all cultures to come in to participate, and a lot of people didn't want that and left the congregation. I had some dark and miserable days back then, but then I remembered Psalm 118:24, and it changed my attitude.

Whoa! I told myself. *This is the day that the Lord has made. I will rejoice and be glad in it.* I started declaring that truth every day, and my mindset progressed from there. *Why have bad days at all?* I thought. *I can have a bad hour, even a bad minute, but never a bad day.*

Since then, I've chosen to never give in to disappointment and be sorry for an entire day. So, I gave each day a special name that I call, sign, and profess. For example, I call Sunday "Super Sunday." I sign it that day by using "Super Sunday" in my electronic messages. I profess it by saying "It's a Super Sunday" aloud throughout the day. I also came up with Marvelous Monday, Terrific Tuesday, Wonderful Wednesday, Triumphant Thursday, Fantastic Friday, and Successful Saturday!

These started out as nothing more than titles, but I have since developed attributes, characteristics, and principles to go with each one, creating material to teach and preach from these concepts. As a result, my self-motivation technique has become a powerful way to motivate others.

In the end, a positive organizational climate is created through leaders and team members who are internally aware of their emotions and those of others, and who are able to understand what is happening inside the organization with its business potential and people. As we develop new levels of mental and emotional self-management through a God-A-Tude of Emotional Intelligence, we become more productive, more creative, and more responsive to the particular needs of others and our organization. Unless they create an environment that fosters mental and emotional balance by providing the information and motivation needed to help their people develop new self-management skills, organizations cannot expect to see long-term sustainable success in today's social and business world.

Of course, a reality that both individuals and companies deal with on an ongoing basis is money management. Our attitude toward money should be one of mission and purpose.

Money is not just to spend, but to be a tool for life improvement—as we'll see in the next God-A-Tude.

4

GOD-A-TUDE OF MONEY

Money is a resource.
God is the source.

The O'Jays sang about it back in the day: *Money, money, money, money—money!* They lamented of the drawbacks and hailed the benefits of the almighty dollar on society, and rightly concluded that "money can drive some people out of their minds!"

Everyone needs it, some want lots of it, and many love it, but far fewer people have a proper attitude, a God-A-Tude, about it. I totally believe that we can have millions, even billions, of dollars if we work hard for it—and the more money we have, the more we can do to help make a difference in this world.

According to the Bible, it is a fact that God has promised to bless those who trust in Him with wealth and prosperity, but many people, including Christians, never obtain God's promise because of their self-centered attitude toward the blessing of finances. We must learn to look at money in the same respect that God does—as a resource to get things done and make a positive difference.

What is money for?

Many people want God to bless them so that they may be rich, have plenty, and never have to use their faith in God. With all of their financial and material needs fulfilled, they'll never be in need, and therefore will never have to turn to God as their provider.

Yet we must understand that anything we do outside of faith is sin (Romans 14:23). Even the millionaire who acknowledges Jesus Christ as Lord of his life must continue to use his faith to go higher with his life's aspirations and in attaining the spiritual things of God. In addition, Job 36:11 teaches that if we obey and serve the Lord, we shall spend our "days in prosperity" and our "years in pleasures." But notice that the prosperity and pleasures only come with obedience and service.

Deuteronomy 8:13-18 clearly communicates God's attitude about money.

"When your herds and your flocks increase, and your silver and gold increase, and everything that you have increases, then your heart will become proud and you will forget the Lord your God who brought you out of the land of Egypt, out of the house of slavery; He who led you through the great and terrible wilderness, with its fiery serpents and scorpions, and its thirsty ground where there was no water; He who brought water for you out of the rock of flint. In the wilderness it was He who fed you manna which your fathers did not know, in order to humble you and in order to put you to the test, to do good for you in the end. Otherwise, you may say in your heart, 'My power and the strength of my hand made me this wealth.'

But you are to remember the Lord your God, for it is He who is giving you power to make wealth, in order to confirm His covenant which He swore to your fathers, as it is this day."

So, what does this passage tell us about money? First, it affirms God's promise to provide for us, which is proven by what He does and through the opportunities that He gives us to use money for good. Second, it is a reminder that money is provided by God so that we may use it wisely, not selfishly. We are enabled to use money properly only because of the ability and efficiency that God has given to us to do so.

God is our one and only source for everything in life—so when we start to trust in money as our source instead of a resource He has provided, we denounce the true power and dominion of God.

Because of the systematic cycle we face each day, particularly in the workplace, it can be easy as employees or leaders to subconsciously begin placing our confidence, or faith, in how our work provides the money we need, but we must avoid this tendency. Dr. I.V. Hilliard declared five things that should alert us that we have put our trust in money instead of God:

> God is our one and only source for everything in life.

1. **When my worth and esteem is determined by what I possess.** There was a young, up-and-coming man who believed that his importance came from the things he possessed. In fact, the more he bought, the better he felt about himself. He had a mentor who saw his potential and took the time to talk to him about developing

a mindset of self-worth that came from God and was centered around principles of hard work and dedication. That God-A-Tude of self-esteem redefined how he thought about himself, brought new purpose to his life, and helped him to see God, not money, as His source.

2. **When a change in my financial state causes a change in how I treat others.** After securing a promotion, a company leader began treating his fellow team members disrespectfully. He looked down on everyone and didn't even acknowledge some of them. He made decisions without asking others on his team how they felt about it because he believed he was the big man in town.

   Not until a true friend challenged his attitude of disrespect and taught him about servant leadership (see next chapter) did he realize that what he was doing was wrong. The leader was a smart guy who had great skills, but people follow others not because of their wits, charisma, or status, but because they trust and believe in that person. He developed a God-A-Tude where he put others first, and everything changed—including his misplaced confidence in money to define who he was and how he behaved.

3. **When I begin to rationalize why I should not give what I should.** There was a young lady who had been giving regularly to charitable organizations from her monthly pay. However, after a large sum of money was awarded to her, she decided that she had given enough and wanted to keep all of it for herself. She was challenged by her father, one of my colleagues. He reminded her God had been good to her and that she'd been doing

some good things, but that God would continue to bless her only as she blessed Him. He pointed his daughter to biblical principles that encouraged rather than corrected her, and she chose to reinstate her practice of giving and renewed her focus on God, not money, as her source.

4. **When I choose to violate godly principles to gain money.** An organization that was doing well in its particular industry had an opportunity to gain more market share—but that chance was compromised when an annual audit of its operations and finances revealed some problems. The operations audit looked at what the organization did to ensure that it was following guidelines and principles for that industry, while the financial audit was designed to make sure the company's money was being allocated properly and that everything was on the straight and narrow taxwise. The organization's money was being so severely and fraudulently mismanaged that the CEO was fired, and new leadership was brought in to reinstate principles of responsibility and accountability from a godly perspective.

5. **When my financial state is valued above my obedience to God.** When someone esteems what's in their pocketbook over what's in God's book, then their attitude about money is in error. Wanting to use money as a power source—to buy friendships or to maneuver and deceive people—instead of as a resource, reveals greed and self-centeredness. Scripture teaches us to "seek first" the Kingdom of God and His righteousness, and as we do, "all these things," meaning all of our monetary

and material necessities for life, "will be provided" or added on for us (Matthew 6:33). God is the source, and the money He provides is the resource.

The proper philosophy about money

You'll recall that philosophy is "loving the way we think," and that God wants us to live with a philosophy that is seen from His heavenly perspective, not the world's earthly viewpoint.

In the book of Ecclesiastes, Solomon—whom the Bible says was given wealth and honor from God that were without equal in his time (1 Kings 3:13)—taught us God's perspective about wealth in a section of Scripture entitled "The Foolishness of Riches."

"One who loves money will not be satisfied with money, nor one who loves abundance with its income. This too is futility. When good things increase, those who consume them increase. So what is the advantage to their owners except to look at them? The sleep of the laborer is sweet, whether he eats little or much; but the full stomach of the rich person does not allow him to sleep." (Ecclesiastes 5:10-12)

Monetary wealth can bring anxiety, so Solomon finished that chapter by concluding that man should find fulfillment in whatever lot he finds himself. Paul expounded on that point in 1 Timothy 6:6-8. He wrote, "But godliness actually is a means of great gain when accompanied by contentment. For we have brought nothing into the world, so we cannot take anything out of it, either. If we have food and covering, with these we shall be content."

The foolishness of riches is quite real. Foolishness is defined as a lack of good judgement—and many people lack wisdom about the purpose of money. When we don't know the purpose of something, abuse is inevitable. We may spend all we gain for personal pleasure rather than engage in delayed gratification, which is an essential practice to being a good steward that brings stability and prosperity in the long run. I knew a couple who received a large tax refund. Instead of saving some, or most, of that money to pay off bills and invest a portion of it, they spent all of it on household improvements. That choice wasn't bad in and of itself, but if they had better discerned how to use the refund, perhaps they could've reduced their debt while making some minor improvements on their home.

When we prioritize money, it becomes our little god that can grow into a really big god. We end up looking for satisfaction from something that has no power to truly satisfy. Paul continued his instruction to Timothy about money by saying, "Those who want to get rich fall into temptation and a trap, and many foolish and harmful desires which plunge people into ruin and destruction. For the love of money is a root of all sorts of evil, and some by longing for it have wandered away from the faith and pierced themselves with many griefs." (1 Timothy 6:9-10)

Many times, when we fall in love with money, we also fall in love with compromise and suffer the loss of our integrity. That also leads us to lose focus on the mission and destiny that God has given us. We open our minds to a world of destructive behavior that plunge us into the deep. Paul added, "As for the rich in this present world, instruct them not to be conceited and arrogant, nor to set their hope on the uncertainty of riches, but on God, who richly and ceaselessly provides us with everything for our enjoyment." (1 Timothy 6:17, AMP) We must focus on God and enjoy life and His creation, not money itself. There is a difference between enjoying the life God has given us—living the abundant life (John 10:10)—and enjoying money.

Finally, while nice houses, automobiles, jewelry, or fancy clothing have their place for enjoyment in our lives, God gave us the power to get wealth *for the establishment of His covenant* (Deuteronomy 8:18). What does that mean? His covenant—His promise to redeem humanity—is established as we use our money to fund ministry work that accomplishes that purpose. Money is for the mission!

As believers in God, we are to feed the hungry, clothe the naked, and provide shelter for those who have no place to sleep. We are to provide education for those less fortunate than ourselves, giving them an opportunity to be in an environment geared for success. Money is needed to achieve all of these needs—and each one helps to fulfill God's covenant.

There is a great organization I have worked with over the years in Honduras that builds schools, feeds the poor, and trains individuals to make a productive living. I made several trips to Honduras with this organization, doing everything from field work to leadership training. In Genesis 12:1-3, Abram (later renamed Abraham) was told by God that He would bless him to be a blessing. When the Lord blesses us financially, it is never just for us. A company in our area that does work for the Department of Defense won a significant contract which considerably increased their revenue. It took over $100,000 of that increase to be a blessing to an area non-profit organization that takes care of orphans.

Two cautionary tales

During His ministry on earth, Jesus spoke to people using parables— simple stories used to illustrate a moral or a spiritual lesson. In one such tale, Christ solidified God's philosophy about money. Called the "Parable of the Rich Fool," it is found in Luke 12:13-21.

"Now someone in the crowd said to Him [Jesus], 'Teacher, tell my brother to divide the family inheritance with me.' But He said to him, 'You there—who appointed Me a judge or arbitrator over the two of you?' But He said to them, 'Beware, and be on your guard against every form of greed; for not even when one is affluent does his life consist of his possessions.' And He told them a parable, saying, 'The land of a rich man was very productive. And he began thinking to himself, saying, "What shall I do, since I have no place to store my crops?" And he said, "This is what I will do: I will tear down my barns and build larger ones, and I will store all my grain and my goods there. And I will say to myself, 'You have many goods stored up for many years to come; relax, eat, drink, and enjoy yourself!'" But God said to him, 'You fool! This very night your soul is demanded of you; and as for all that you have prepared, who will own it now?' Such is the one who stores up treasure for himself, and is not rich in relation to God."

When we love money, we lose sight of the big picture. We must have a God-A-Tude that God is our source, not what we have in the bank or stuffed away under the mattress. The wise person keeps a solid relationship with God, enjoying life every day. Our peace is not found in money or things, but in our faith in God.

> When we love money, we lose sight of the big picture.

In the second story, Jesus was approached by a rich young ruler who "ran up to Him and knelt before Him, and asked Him, 'Good Teacher, what shall I do so that I may inherit eternal life?' But Jesus said to him, 'Why do you call Me good? No one is good except God alone. You know the commandments: "Do not murder, Do not commit adultery, Do not steal, Do not give false testimony, Do not defraud, Honor your father and mother." And he said to Him, 'Teacher, I have kept all these things from my youth.' Looking at him, Jesus showed love to him and said to him, 'One thing you lack: go and sell all you possess and give to the poor, and you will have treasure in heaven; and come, follow Me.' But he was deeply dismayed by these words, and he went away grieving; for he was one who owned much property." (Mark 10:17-22)

The young man's attitude about being great in life was all about his actions, not his heart. His heart was with his money. The account concluded, "And Jesus, looking around, said to His disciples, 'How hard it will be for those who are wealthy to enter the kingdom of God!' And the disciples were amazed at His words. But Jesus responded again and said to them, 'Children, how hard it is to enter the kingdom of God! It is easier for a camel to go through the eye of a needle than for a rich person to enter the kingdom of God.' And they were even more astonished, and said to Him, 'Then who can be saved?' Looking at them, Jesus said, 'With people it is impossible, but not with God; for all things are possible with God.'" (Mark 10:23-27)

During His Sermon on the Mount, Jesus instructed, "Do not store up for yourselves treasures on earth, where moth and rust destroy, and where thieves break in and steal. But store up for yourselves treasures in heaven, where neither moth nor rust destroys, and where thieves do not break in or steal; for where your treasure is, there your heart will be also ... No one can serve two masters; for either he will hate the one and love the other, or he will be devoted to one and despise the other. You cannot serve God and wealth." (Matthew 6:19-21, 24)

It is clear. God has blessed each one of us with the ability to make money, and He desires for us to prosper—but it's not for ourselves. A God-A-Tude of Money requires us to use a significant portion of what we earn to fund or do His work, fulfilling His covenant. It all starts with discerning how we can use what He provides as our source to be a resource to help others in ways that glorify Him.

As we develop our God-A-Tudes—attitudes based on the Word of God that brings success in life—with our confidence, our emotional intelligence, and with our money, we are then positioned to be leaders in our society, our workplaces, and our homes.

It is an incredible responsibility, and our success is predicated on following the right example.

5

GOD-A-TUDE OF A SUCCESSFUL LEADER

Look out for other people and put them first.

In his book, *The Spirit of Leadership: Cultivating the Attributes That Influence Human Action,* evangelist and leadership consultant Dr. Myles Munroe defined leadership as "the capacity to influence others through inspiration, motivated by a passion, generated by a vision, produced by a conviction, and ignited by a purpose." Pastor, speaker, and leadership expert John C. Maxwell simply said, "leadership is influence, nothing more, nothing less."

No one else exemplified these definitions and modeled the God-A-Tude of a Successful Leader better than Jesus Christ. Through His example, we discover that servant leadership is the key to being victorious and successful. At the beginning of His ministry, Jesus quoted the prophet Isaiah and stated this about Himself. "The Spirit of the Lord is upon Me, because He has anointed Me to bring good news to the poor. He has sent Me to proclaim release to captives, and recovery of sight to the blind, to set free those who are oppressed, to proclaim the favorable year of the Lord." (Luke 4:18-19)

In that passage, Christ expressed how He was going to use His life as a leader to focus on serving others. Perhaps the greatest example of this from His incredible life is found in John 13 during the Passover feast when Christ went to His knees before each one of His disciples and washed their dirty feet. A menial task usually performed by a servant when guests arrived at a home, this surprising Divine foot washing was done deliberately during the meal to emphasize a lesson of selfless service that Jesus had exemplified throughout His short but world-changing public ministry. Later during that same meal, in response to a debate among the disciples about who was the greatest, Christ said, "But I am among you as the one who serves." (Luke 22:27).

Helping others win

Mark Miller, the vice president of High Performance Leadership at Chick-Fil-A, elaborated on godly servant leadership in his book, *The Heart of Leadership: Becoming a Leader People Want to Follow.* He wrote, "Servant leadership is an approach contrary to conventional leadership in which the leader's focus is on himself and what he can accomplish and achieve. Rather, the focus is on those being served." While Miller said servant leaders do many of the same things other leaders do, such as cast vision and build teams, the big difference is their orientation and motivation. "They possess an others-first mindset. The servant leader constantly works to help others win."

I once hired a female leader who had a lot of potential to be a great executive. She possessed talent in decision making, change management, and team building. She had a big drive for excellence. She wanted to be the best and to help as much as possible, and she was on board with the vision that I had cast for the company. Her ceiling of advancement was high, so I set aside time to become a mentor to her. We discussed improvement in areas such as people skills and in having over-all wisdom when making executive decisions. The time I dedicated to her was taken from time that I could have been doing things for myself, but I decided to put her future first. She was a very open-minded mentee who took to heart everything she learned. Within three years, she had advanced in her career and currently serves as our vice president of operations.

Servant leadership also works because it honors others—acknowledging their different roles, responsibilities, and strengths. As Miller put it, "It is not about who's in charge. It's about who is responsible for what, and how can I, as the leader, help people be successful."

A super guy who possessed the rare talents of negotiation and conflict resolution came into my circle when we sat on

> Servant leadership works because it honors others.

the same non-profit board. Immediately recognizing his gifting, I hired him to fulfill a few specific roles to help take my organization to another level, first as a consultant and later as a staff member. I acknowledged his strengths and put them to use in various ways—and he told me it was his confidence in my leadership philosophy that helped him to grow and be able to improve those around him. In that philosophy, I allow people to fail and learn from their mistakes, all while knowing that I have their backs. It was something he had never seen in other leaders, and it allowed him to have a safe place to mature and allow his talents to flourish. It continues to be a joy to watch him work and grow.

Leaders who are servants don't blame others. They own their actions and their outcomes. This speaks to accountability where leaders praise others on their team when they do well and take full responsibility for the good or bad outcomes of the team. Ability Plus is an organization with many moving parts that is monitored by strict state rules. We are subject to an annual audit from the state that requires us to accept auditors who have different personalities and want things done in various formats. Therefore, we often have to go to our house managers and other staff during the audit period with demands that can bring great stress to our entire team.

In 2021, during our annual review from the state regarding the services we provide, we were cited in several areas, and the auditor went over all the improvements needed for our organization to be in full compliance. Instead of blaming my team for the problems at hand, I told the auditors that the issues were my responsibility as CEO and that we would address them and move to a positive status. I promised to personally oversee the process to the end. It's difficult to take responsibility instead of passing it on to others, but it's always best to be proactive rather than reactive. I asked myself, "What did I do to help them get their job done?" "Did I do everything I could to help them?" "Was I as fully supportive as I needed to be?" This type of accountability helps me to get better and to know the strengths and weaknesses of those who follow me on my team.

Finally, servant leaders are men and women who see things *that could be*—and Miller pointed out that the future they see is always a better version of the present. "We believe we can make a difference; we think we can make the world, or at least our part of it, better," he said. When I took over Ability Plus, the company was in big trouble from a financial, structural, and cultural viewpoint. As a servant leader, I addressed the team to let them know that we were going to be better in the future. I did not have all the answers or the resources, but I had the mindset to roll up my sleeves and get to work with a determination to motivate others to do the same. I told the staff that I would not ask them to do anything that I wasn't willing to do myself. They saw me get up every day and stay in the fight with them. I told them often that I appreciated what they did. I told them we would learn as we went. We all leaned on each other's strengths—and we turned things around.

Foundational God-A-Tudes of great leadership

Leaders think differently about themselves. That is what distinguishes them from followers. I've identified seven God-A-Tudes that are foundational to great leadership. Some of these attitudes may be more present in the personality of one leader than another, but each of these attitudes can be strengthened. Whether they naturally possess these qualities or not, great leaders are diligent to consistently develop each one of these God-A-Tudes for their unique leadership roles.

1. A great leader has exemplary character

Miller wrote of leadership being like an iceberg: 10 percent above the waterline and about 90 percent below. The part above the water indicates leadership skills, but the rest below represents leadership character. "If you want to predict people's ultimate success as leaders," Miller said, "evaluate not their skills but their leadership character."

It is of utmost importance that leaders are trustworthy. They should be known to live with honestly and integrity. Great leaders "walk the talk," earning the right to have responsibility for others as they do. Servant leadership builds trust simply because we trust leaders whose motives are centered around others. True authority is born out of the respect and trustworthiness shown by great leaders.

> It is of utmost importance that leaders are trustworthy.

Titus 2:7-8 says, "In all things show yourself to be an example of good deeds, with purity in doctrine, dignified, sound in speech which is beyond reproach, so that the opponent will be put to shame, having nothing bad to say about us." Dr. Maurice K. Wright, my spiritual mentor, embodied this verse and the character it described. In his role as general overseer and visionary of United Christian Church in Gadsden, Alabama, I saw firsthand how Dr. Wright carried himself as a leader, treating everyone with respect and dignity. He worked hard for the cause of Christianity to better others, not to gain a name for himself. His character encouraged me and others to always strive to serve in a way that glorified God and grew His Kingdom.

Dr. Wright was like a father to me, and I would definitely describe myself as a disciple of his. I will miss him; he passed away in April 2020.

Regarding character, Hebrews 13:5 exhorts, "Make sure that your character is free from the love of money, being content with what you have; for He Himself has said, 'I will never desert you, nor will I ever abandon you.'" Servant leaders should be people of fiscal responsibility and, when needed, monetary sacrifice. While working as CEO of Ability Plus, I received an offer to take a job that would've tripled my annual salary and provided other attractive benefits. It was an incredible opportunity, but after prayer and counsel from people such as Dr. Wright, I decided that purpose, not money, should be the criteria to take the position. When we chase our purpose and passion, money will follow. Money is not the endgame. I turned down the offer to remain in my purpose and passion at Ability Plus, knowing that when you walk in your purpose, you are walking in you.

2. A great leader is enthusiastic about their work, ministry, or cause, as well as about their role as a leader

It's undeniable that people will respond more openly to a person of passion and dedication. Leaders need to be a source of inspiration and a motivator toward the required action or cause. Although the responsibilities and roles of each one of these leaders may be different, they need to be part of the team, unafraid to roll up their sleeves and get dirty. These leaders are mentioned by Paul in 2 Corinthians 9:2. "For I know your willingness, of which I boast about you to the Macedonians, namely, that Achaia has been prepared since last year, and your zeal has stirred up most of them."

Early in my career as a pastor, my first church was a young ministry that was growing at a constant rate. That meant our initial facility was not sufficient for us to have the programs and outreaches we wanted for the community. So, I found an old warehouse that had a lot of potential but was quite run down. It needed a ton of work, but I was enthusiastic about what we could do with the building.

As an engineer, I mentally drew up my plans for it and communicated them to my church leadership team. We got the property, remodeled it, and used it for the next three years. The highlight was the summer youth program that it allowed us to facilitate. After moving into the building, one of my elders revealed that, in reality, the leadership team didn't see anything that I saw in my mind, but my enthusiasm caused them to follow my recommendation to acquire the building.

3. A great leader is confident

In order to set direction, leaders need to be confident as individuals and in their leadership role. Such a person inspires confidence in others and draws out the trust of the team to complete the task well. A leader who conveys confidence toward the proposed objective brings out the best in all those around them. In the Bible, Paul wrote, "For I am confident of this very thing, that He who began a good work among you will complete it by the day of Christ Jesus." (Philippians 1:6) That "good work" includes being confident through Christ in our vocation and in our abilities as leaders.

When I started doing leadership consulting through Vision Excellence Company, I didn't know anyone who had started such a company. Yet I felt that the Lord had put this vision in my heart and that He wanted me to exercise my confidence and faith in Him. Within three months of moving forward, God opened up two doors of opportunity to consult with two different organizations. I didn't have all the know-how I needed, but I did know that the Lord was with me, and my total confidence was in Him. That humble beginning has developed into a team providing seminars, training, and coaching in a dozen different strategic areas to help individuals and organizations lead, innovate, and grow.

4. A great leader functions in an orderly and purposeful manner during times of uncertainty

People look to their leaders during transition or turmoil. They will find reassurance and security when leaders portray a positive demeanor in trial or difficulty. In 2 Chronicles 20, Jehoshaphat faced great uncertainty as the nation of Judah faced a vast army, a Moabite alliance, on the warpath with every intention of destroying his kingdom. Jehoshaphat cried out to God, "we are powerless before this great multitude that is coming against us; nor do we know what to do, but our eyes are on You." (2 Chronicles 20:11) Then, after the people of Judah prayed, fasted, and sought the direction of God, the Lord spoke through the prophet Jahaziel, saying, "This is what the Lord says: Do not be afraid! Don't be discouraged by this mighty army, for the battle is not yours, but God's." (2 Chronicles 20:15, NLT)

As a member of the advisory board for the business school at Alabama A&M University, I was tasked with serving on a committee to assist the dean, faculty, and staff to achieve international accreditation. There were many requirements to get the certification, and we could not be distracted with others' opinions about how hard it was going to be to achieve that status. The dean was a fearless leader who kept every meeting and work session in line with order and purpose. He made sure everyone knew before each meeting what was going to be talked about, and he provided the background information we needed so we would be prepared to discuss next steps to achieve the accreditation.

It took two years, but we got it done. That international accreditation serves to protect the interests of the university's students, their parents, the institution, and potential employers by ensuring that the educational programs offered have attained a level that meets or exceeds standards that were developed by experts in their fields.

5. A great leader is tolerant of ambiguity and remains calm, composed, and steadfast to the main purpose

Storms, emotions, and crises come and go—and great leaders take these as part of the journey and keeps a cool head in the midst of them. In 1 Corinthians 15:58, Paul says to "be firm, immovable, always excelling in the work of the Lord, knowing that your labor is not in vain in the Lord."

During the 2021 audit of Ability Plus that I mentioned earlier, the state representative asked to see our procedures for tracking the behaviors of our clients. These behaviors can include acting out, a response to a medical treatment, or a deterioration in their overall condition. We had recorded this information using a form the state representative didn't like or understand—so we had no other choice than to change our form and tracking procedures to fit the representative's request. We had to take the information we had, put it into the new form, and then make sure the procedures read the way the state wanted. This took weeks, and to say the least, was not appealing to our team. But we reminded one another to stay calm under pressure.

6. A great leader is able to think analytically and stay focused on the goal

Not only do great leaders view a situation as a whole, but they are able to break it down into subparts for closer inspection. Not only is the end goal in view, but it can be broken down into manageable steps so that progress can be made. As the Bible declares, "The simple believes everything, but the prudent gives thought to his steps." (Proverbs 14:15, ESV)

When I launched Vision Excellence Company, I had a goal of becoming more involved in the community because I wanted to increase my influence among senior leaders in northern Alabama. After receiving advice on how to proceed with this goal, I developed a plan to achieve it that focused on leading with purpose and making a difference in the community. It couldn't be done all at once, so I had to exercise patience along the way as each step required a different level of maturity.

First, I established a relationship and partnership with the local Chamber of Commerce. Second, I started to support community charities by attending several of their monthly and annual events. Third, I served on the boards of six different non-profit organizations in the region. This led to me being asked to be part of several key groups of influence, helping me to learn and grow from other leaders throughout the area. I was allowed to offer my advice and guidance to address issues from workforce development and diversity and inclusion matters to annual fundraising campaigns and providing leader mentorship. In all, it took four years to achieve my goal, and I not only met my expectations, but I exceeded them.

7. A great leader is committed to excellence

Second best does not lead to success. Great leaders not only maintain high standards, but they are proactive in raising the bar in order to achieve excellence in all areas. In the Old Testament, Daniel was like this. "Then this Daniel distinguished himself above the governors and satraps, because an excellent spirit was in him; and the king gave thought to setting him over the whole realm." (Daniel 6:3, NKJV)

When the COVID-19 pandemic hit our world in 2020, many companies, churches, and organizations had to start operating in different ways. This included doing more with technology and media. At my church, we had to turn to live streaming as the main source of ministry programming to our members. We had already been doing a live stream, but it was only as a second option to in-person attendance and participation. We realized we had to deliver a better and improved virtual experience as the pandemic kept most people at home.

> Second best does not lead to success.

I got our leadership together with our IT and media team to create a plan to produce a live streaming broadcast of excellence. This required all of us working together not just on technical changes, but also on how we conducted worship and services. Everyone got on board, and the response was overwhelmingly positive. Workers, volunteers, and congregants had an attitude of success. Those watching the stream liked the upgraded cameras, the new backdrop, and how the IT department placed Bible scriptures on the screen. This commitment to excellence caused everyone to look at what they were doing and ask how they could do it better.

As a pastor, I had always hoped that I had been able to transfer an attitude of excellence to the church in general, but you never really know until a stressor comes and change happens. It was fulfilling to see the fruit of everything I had poured into my staff and congregation as their shepherd and their leader realized.

All of us need to be successful leaders—and that God-A-Tude requires us to look out for other people and put them first. In order to put others first, we need to be part of a team. Each one of us accomplishes more when we're in it together.

No leader does anything on their own. They don't take credit on their own. They don't turn the company around on their own. They don't make progress on their own. It takes a team with everybody doing their part and operating in their expertise—and that's what we'll talk about next.

6

GOD-A-TUDE OF TEAMWORK

All devoted to one. One devoted to all.
That is what makes up an effective team.

I first learned how to build an effective cohesive leadership team not in business, but as a pastor. When my wife and I launched Emmanuel The Connection Church in 1996, we immediately recognized that we needed a team to succeed in our vision of saving and empowering people. The mission was too big for a couple of people to achieve. More than that, we did not want to be just another building on the corner with a name on it. We wanted our church to make a real difference in the Huntsville community.

We had all these ideas of what we wanted to do, but we had to plan, discuss, and agree upon who was going to do what, when they were going to do it, and how they were going to get it done. We had to be on the same page. It was a challenge because we had some people who had left other ministries to be a part of ours, and each one came to us with different titles, roles, and abilities. We had to help them understand our vision and how their gifts fit into making it come to pass.

We started by teaching the team about giftings and talents to find out their strengths. Next, we laid out the specific ministries and outreaches we wanted to do, and we assessed where everyone fit best. We took it one step at a time and asked everybody to be a team player.

It took a year-and-a-half to get where we needed to be, but we did it—and our church indeed had a phenomenal impact because we worked as a team.

Essential elements of teamwork

In whatever setting you operate, there is no substitute for having a God-A-Tude of Teamwork. The biblical principle for this God-A-Tude is first presented in 1 Corinthians 12 in Paul's discourse about the use of spiritual gifts.

"Now there are varieties of gifts, but the same Spirit. And there are varieties of ministries, and the same Lord. There are varieties of effects, but the same God who works all things in all persons. But to each one is given the manifestation of the Spirit for the common good ... For just as the body is one and yet has many parts, and all the parts of the body, though they are many, are one body, so also is Christ. For by one Spirit we were all baptized into one body, whether Jews or Greeks, whether slaves or free, and we were all made to drink of one Spirit. For the body is not one part, but many." (1 Corinthians 12:4-7, 12-14)

First, **support of one another** is critical in teamwork. The "body," or the entire group of people who make up the team, are not supported by one person, but by each other. They are "one" and are stronger together operating on the same plan. Teamwork is the key to achieving our dreams and, from a spiritual perspective, to accomplishing God's will.

Second, it is very important that each person on the team **know their roles.** Just as the many cultures of the world have their great followers and leaders, each team has great players, some who are destined to succeed individually, and others who are called to be leaders and will take their team to higher places. Whatever their role, each member of the team relies on the other. Ephesians 4:11-13 spells out this principle. Speaking of God, it tells us, "He gave some as apostles, some as prophets, some as evangelists, some as pastors and teachers, for the equipping of the saints for the work of ministry, for the building up of the body of Christ; until we all attain to the unity of the faith."

Unity is the last essential element of teamwork. Unity is the glue that keeps everyone moving in the same direction for a common cause. Without unity, talents and gifts will find themselves in an unproductive state. As 1 Corinthians 1:10 affirms, "I appeal to you, dear brothers and sisters, by the authority of our Lord Jesus Christ, to live in harmony with each other. Let there be no divisions in the church. Rather, be of one mind, united in thought and purpose." (NLT)

The biggest challenge to unity is making sure each person understands their goals and their roles in achieving those goals, then ensuring that every team member put aside their individual egos. It is not about how I want to do it. It is about what needs to be done for the goal to be achieved. Many times, people have their own unique takes on how to get there, but there is a right way defined by our values and culture. Recognizing individuality and giftings to maximize them, then translating them in the team to the mission and purpose, is the key. They have to see how their individual goals are wrapped up in

75

the overall goal so they can still achieve what they want, but to the benefit of the entire team.

In the end, no organization can be healthy without unity. I know that's a bold statement, but it is made after years of experience. When unification is absent in a team, individual gifts, talents, and egos begin to war against each other. The project, process, and plans are ultimately destroyed, and the organization dies. I recall a statewide alliance of leaders that wanted to share in community projects and meet the needs of those less fortunate. But because of their lack of unity from a structural and organizational position, they failed, even after several attempts at trying to right the ship. They couldn't decide who was going to lead, and they did not have a clear mission or vision statement. In addition, they never pinpointed their overall "why." They knew they needed to exist, but they never got to their purpose.

> **No organization can be healthy without unity.**

On the other hand, there was an organization in Georgia that brought leaders together for training, empowerment, and collaboration, and it thrived. Each year, additional leaders from around the country joined their effort, and they had a positive impact on thousands of people. In their case, the leader had a clear vision and mission, precise objectives that he wanted to achieve, and everybody got on board. There was uncompromising unity, and that unity prompted growth and results.

Organizational effectiveness = team cohesiveness

The word "team" is often overused in the sense that we usually refer to any group with more than one person as a team. But a true team is not just two or more people, but a group that is moving in the same direction to accomplish a goal or mission. This necessitates cohesiveness—and there are three ways, when evaluating an organization, that team cohesiveness will bring about overall effectiveness.

1. Building the team. An organization needs a team that works well together. Functional, cross-functional, and self-managing teams are the three different types of teams found within an organization, and each team has its own specific goals and objectives. Functional teams are the traditional teams that generally have a lot of oversight and are in the same discipline: they are all engineers or accountants. Cross-functional teams have members from several disciplines, possibly including someone from marketing or human resources, working to achieve a particular goal. Self-managing teams come up with new ideas on their own. Management has approved this team's work in advance, and its members are not afraid to explore, act, and then present their results to executive leadership.

By resolving conflicts, brainstorming new solutions, initializing innovation, and providing a supportive and encouraging environment for all of these teams, you will improve the performance of individual team members and the organization as a whole. One of the greatest ways to do this is through team building activities. As you provide ample opportunities for the members of your team to interact with and get to know one another, they learn to trust and depend on each other and care for one another. Outdoor physical activities such as a Ropes Course or other obstacle courses are fun ways to learn to work together. I also recommend seminars where team role playing exercises are used to hone communication and collaboration skills.

2. Establishing a goal pyramid. To create an efficient system for achieving goals and making viable progress in a timely manner, do what ancient architects did: create an unshakable structure with at least three levels—company goals, team goals, and individual goals. This goal pyramid starts with your ultimate vision at the very top, followed by team goals at the middle level, and individual tasks and objectives on the bottom. It is a fantastic tool to foster unity, provide transparency, and keep your employees from getting sidetracked from the predetermined road to success. Setting clear objectives on each level is a phenomenal way to measure progress, keep the operation's big-picture goals at the forefront of everyone's minds, and map out a way for every team member to contribute to the larger vision of the organization.

The goal pyramid is created with the executive team looking at the vision and mission statement from one-year, five-year, and 10-year perspectives, and then building company goals for each team and drilling down to establish team goals and what each person needs to do to accomplish those goals. The pyramid is first presented to the team in a group "lunch and learn" setting where they can get fired up, excited, and motivated. It is then shared in detail with team leaders and, through them, to each individual. This is exactly the type of work we do with our clients through Vision Excellence Company.

3. Fostering transparency. There is no better way to accomplish flawless team cohesion than by leading your crew with complete transparency. Business management expert and author Patrick Lencioni refers to this as "getting naked" in his book about client loyalty. It is vital to take the time to enlighten every member on goals, procedures, and policies while setting crystal clear objectives so that each member knows how they are expected to contribute to the overall success of the company. Leading with complete transparency provides everyone with a clear understanding of what they're working toward and how they can support the greater good of the organization. Never punish anyone for being transparent. In fact, you want to provide tips and guidance to encourage transparency and reward people for being transparent.

Integrity is required to establish and solidify transparency. Lencioni wrote that integrity is healthy when it is whole, consistent, and complete—meaning that operations, strategy, and culture all fit together and make sense. I've discovered that integrity can be further defined as the state of being honest and undivided. When operations are doing things in an honest way to support the overall strategic plan that encompasses the established culture, organizational health is achieved. Transparency mandates telling the truth, even if it hurts or costs you something. When you start compromising and not telling the truth, it becomes easier to do, and it infects the culture. Owning up to mistakes might be tough, but it is always the right thing to do.

Five key behaviors of effective teamwork

A *Chicago Tribune* article once told the story of Chad Kreuter, a reserve catcher for the Chicago White Sox, who severely dislocated and fractured his left shoulder on a play at home plate. He underwent surgery, and the White Sox placed him on the 60-day disabled list. That's exactly the kind of thing that can make a backup player feel even less like a part of the team.

But quite the opposite happened. Chad's teammates had a strong liking for him, so each one put Chad's uniform number 12 on his ball cap to show support. This gesture made Chad feel like he was a part of the team even though he couldn't play. Later in the season, after Chad was recovered and able to play once again, he showed his appreciation by putting the uniform number of each of his teammates, every one of them, on his cap.[2]

All devoted to one. One devoted to all. That is what makes up an effective team—and that type of devotion to one another is created and nurtured by five key behaviors.

1. Building trust. "It is required of stewards that one be found trustworthy." (1 Corinthians 4:2)

Biblically speaking, a steward is someone who intentionally utilizes and manages all the resources the Lord provides for a specific purpose, God's honor, and the betterment of humanity—but in a business setting, a steward is more specifically defined as someone who uses resources in a systematic, accountable way and is concerned about the sustainability of the organization. This steward manages cash flow, employee relations, innovation, and other parts of the business for the

---

2 Bill Jauss, "Catcher and Sox Both Seriously Hurt," *Chicago Tribune*, July 20, 1996, Sec. 3, p. 10; Steve Rosenbloom, "Hit and Run," *Chicago Tribune*, September 29, 1996, Sec. 3, p. 1.

betterment of the organization, its employees and customers, and any other stakeholders. Successful stewardship begins by building trust within your team.

There are two types of trust. Predictive trust involves knowing how someone on your team will react in a given situation. For example, my consulting firm worked for an insurance company that had an agent who was directed to build positive relationships and interactions with customers who had strong issues and concerns regarding their policies. We predicted that the agent would lose his cool when the customer pushed hard against him—and we were right. He was placed in a coaching program to train him on how to better work with people. He corrected his behavior, improved, and has done well ever since.

Then there is vulnerability-based trust where team members are completely transparent and honest with one another. When teams have this kind of trust, teammates can genuinely say to each other, "I need help," "I messed up," "I can learn from you," or "You are better at that." While working with a government contracting company and conducting Emotional Intelligence training with its staff, it was revealed that people there felt very safe to share their vulnerabilities with their teammates. They were not afraid of being disrespected or marginalized when asking for help or admitting that they had a problem. In the midst of the training, many others around the table started talking about when they had issues, and their teammates and leaders were very receptive. Everyone was on the same page, and there was clear camaraderie in place that improved the culture.

Of course, at the heart of vulnerability is a willingness to abandon self-pride and fear and sacrifice ego for the good of the team. There was a time when I was working with a large nonprofit organization where the executive director showed great vulnerability-based trust. The organization needed a change in culture and mindset to go to the next level, and he had to move past his ego and admit that how he had been leading the organization was not effective. He admitted to being a little off-center when it came to his vision for the future and where the industry was headed. He showed greater care for the business than for his pride, and he allowed others to help him correct his errors and create the culture change.

The main thing that prevents new team members from building trust is the Fundamental Attribution Error. First identified by social psychologist Lee Ross in 1977, this error speaks to our tendency as human beings to attribute the negative or frustrating behaviors of our colleagues to their intentions and personalities while attributing our own negative or frustrating behaviors to environmental factors. I saw this happen one time when a mid-level manager at a particular company exhibited very negative behaviors that were consistently witnessed by her teammates and other peers. The manager was judgmental toward others in the company, even those outside of her department. She took punitive actions when she felt the behavior of others was not in sync with company policies or culture. She made statements that suggested others behaved in a way intended to harm or even destroy the company. Yet when this manager was confronted about her own behaviors, she always attributed them to the systems and conditions she was placed in by management. It wasn't until she received coaching that she recognized what was going on with her and how she affected others. She corrected herself and is still with the company.

In the end, building trust is the first and most important behavior listed because it provides the foundation for all of the others.

2. Mastering conflict. "For to you it has been granted for Christ's sake, not only to believe in Him, but also to suffer on His behalf, experiencing the same conflict which you saw in me, and now hear to be in me." (Philippians 1:29-30)

In this Bible passage, Paul teaches that believers in Jesus are going to experience some suffering and conflict because of their faith in Him. Both are essential to personal development and to being effective in His Kingdom work, and they are a normal part of life. This principle, therefore, seamlessly relates to all of our relationships, including those on a team at work—and that's good because, contrary to popular wisdom, conflict is *not* a bad thing for a team. In fact, when trust is present in a team, conflict becomes nothing else but the pursuit of the truth.

> When trust is present in a team, conflict becomes nothing else but the pursuit of the truth.

I remember working with leaders of an organization where one of the executives had a different idea on how maintenance should carry out its roles in the company. Most of the leaders viewed the maintenance department as being overwhelmed with open tickets to fix everyday problems and felt it needed a separate person to be in charge of long-term preventive maintenance issues. But the one executive felt strongly that the department was simply not managing its time properly and could be more aware and proactive about those long-range issues.

A detailed SWOT analysis (a study undertaken by an organization to identify its internal strengths and weaknesses, as well as its external opportunities and threats) and an on-the-ground evaluation was conducted. It was readily confirmed that the maintenance department did not have enough time to perform as required but could make improvements to better manage the time it had. The conflict resulted in the truth being exposed and the situation was rectified.

On the other hand, conflict without trust becomes politics: an attempt to manipulate others in order to win an argument regardless of the truth. One company had a supervisor who felt it was his personal duty to be in conflict with everyone. He used his position and title to manipulate people to war against one another just to get his point across. Those who worked for him only followed his direction because they were afraid of getting fired. He was eventually let go because his conflict was not healthy for the company. In the end, politicizing is almost always bad and divisive.

Naturally, disagreement during conflict brings with it a level of discomfort even among the most trusting of team members. Overcoming the tendency to run from that discomfort is one of the most important requirements for any team leader, calling to mind the familiar adage, "No pain, no gain." At one organization, there was a team member who was loyal but fed up with her supervisor's manipulative tactics. She was a stellar leader, had endured other politics in the office, and remained solid in her work performance, but she was still planning to leave the company out of frustration. Thankfully, other leadership assured her the executive's behavior would no longer be tolerated, he was removed from the company, and she chose to remain. Ultimately, she was promoted to that former executive's position, and the company is thriving under her leadership. None of it was easy or comfortable, but the result was great gain for everyone.

Avoiding discomfort in conflict only transfers greater quantities of mistrust into more groups of people throughout the organization. It is also true that different people and varying cultures participate in conflict in different ways. In many African American cultures, individuals may raise their voice levels during conversation, which may seem to some to be yelling. But it is actually a normal way they communicate during conflict. It may appear to be hostile and rude when they are in fact showing the highest level of respect for one another. The seemingly aggressive physical gesturing that may accompany such a conversation is not an indication of anger or mistrust, but of conviction of thought. Two people who are engaged in something important and who trust and care for one another should feel free to disagree, sometimes passionately.

This conflict continuum is vital, yet it necessitates the employment of two conflict tools, particularly when there is a strong cultural aversion to the discomfort conflict brings. *Mining for conflict* allows effective team leaders to establish an obligation to show dissent, knowing that if they don't, conversations that should be happening in the open will instead occur in isolated pockets and behind closed doors to the detriment of the team. While it is natural to desire consensus, the more productive approach is to get more people to speak and share their ideas so that ultimately, as Lencioni says, you "avoid the destructive hallway conversations that inevitably result when people are reluctant to engage in direct, productive debate." *Real-time permission* enables team members to coach one another instead of retreating from healthy debate. When people engaged in conflict are becoming uncomfortable with the level of discord, they should be reminded that what they are doing is necessary so they will have the confidence to continue. Once the meeting has ended, it is helpful to remind those participants that the conflict they just experienced was good for the team and not something to avoid.

Cohesive teams must take a few minutes to ensure that everyone understands each other. At the end of one executive board meeting that saw much conflict, the team decided to move forward with an updated strategic plan. Everyone around the table was asked individually if they had an issue or any questions about the new additions. Those were addressed and everyone was supportive of the plan.

3. Achieving commitment. "Commit your works to the Lord, And your plans will be established." (Proverbs 16:3)

Conflict is vital—for a team cannot achieve commitment without it. Good conflict brings out what needs to be done, addresses the why, who, and what, and leads to a goal that the team can commit to and achieve. The only way to prevent bad communication is to arrive at specific agreements. The problem with communication is many times we think we have done it well when we actually did not do a good job of it at all.

There was a time when we were going to conduct our church services a different way by being live in one location while simulcasting it to our headquarter location. I thought I had communicated this thoroughly to everyone, but on the day of the simulcast, several people stayed at home because they thought we were only going to be online. We quickly had to regroup and communicate that everyone should attend services as they normally would, and leadership would provide specifics about the flow of service once they got to the facility.

We also had to reemphasize that worship and all other normal aspects of the service would continue.

At the same time, waiting for consensus in communication before taking action can lead to mediocrity and frustration. One company had a situation where they needed to change how payroll was handled and when they would pay team members. A new vendor had all the tools and support the company needed to make the changes, but not everyone was on board, and some were even fearful they might not get paid on time. So, leadership had the payroll company come in and do a demonstration of the capabilities of the new system and how it would execute and deploy the needed changes. After proper vetting, leadership decided to go forward even though one of the executives in human resources was against it. A beta test was done as a trial with a sample of team members, it worked well, and it brought consensus to the group.

It's only when people see true commitment that they will be positioned to embrace accountability.

4. Embracing accountability. "So then each one of us will give an account of himself to God. Therefore let's not judge one another anymore, but rather determine this: not to put an obstacle or a stumbling block in a brother's or sister's way." (Romans 14:12-13)

To hold someone accountable is to care about them enough to risk having them blame you for pointing out their deficiencies—and on a team, peer-to-peer accountability is the primary and most effective source of being answerable and responsible to one another. I hold myself accountable to those I lead. When there is a new project, initiative, or program that we have said we are going to do, I ask my team to hold my feet to the fire on quality, care, and delivery time of the outcomes.

I developed a program of rewarding team members who did this by recognizing a winner via video each week. This was difficult to do with my very hectic schedule, but I made it happen, and the team benefitted from the program.

On cohesive teams, peers confront one another without having to involve leadership. This avoids distractions and politics. Two mid-level managers of an influential organization had a disagreement concerning the process and the depth of information that should be given to those outside of their cross-function strategy group. One felt that everything discussed should be shared in its entirety. The other believed that only a summary of highlights was necessary. Without going to leadership, they came up with a solution both liked. A general summary was to be shared, with the agreement that if more info was requested, it would be given.

As part of embracing accountability, team leaders must overcome the "wuss" factor. They cannot wimp out when confronting team members on their behavior. I saw this play itself out at a large organization that had a close executive team. An executive had to confront another peer who was not taking accountability for the actions of his team. He had team members who were lagging in their duties, causing his department and others within the company to suffer. The executive told the peer about the issue and challenged him to correct things before the situation escalated and the CEO got involved.

It was hard to do. The executive and his peer had worked together for years and were friends, but in this case, the overall health of the company and its teams was more important than their personal friendship and had to be addressed. In the end, the peer could not deny the problem and truly wanted to do his best for everyone. Even though it was an uncomfortable situation, the person who was doing the offending behavior recognized it and corrected it—and no harm was done to the friendship.

It is important to distinguish between the main forms of accountability. *Measurable* accountability is easier with leaders because there are no gray areas. It is not just based on someone's judgment and theory. Measured accountability is described in specific terms (such as amount and duration) that can be easy seen. At the same time, *behavioral* accountability is more important than measurable accountability because behavioral problems almost always precede performance downturn. Most people's actions don't just show up out of thin air. The behaviors exist, but they may not have yet manifested themselves. Therefore, it is very important to address behaviors in their infancy when proper leadership can gear the individual in the right direction. It should be looked at as a strategic planning objective and addressed as soon as possible. If it isn't, the behaviors will either stay hidden or they will manifest themselves in even worse ways.

5. Focusing on results. "[God], from whom the whole body, being fitted and held together by what every joint supplies, according to the proper working of each individual part, causes the growth of the body for the building up of itself in love." (Ephesians 4:16)

In this passage, Paul is saying that that when we work together while doing what we are supposed to do individually, then we can grow as a team and get the results we expect from our work. As each person takes responsibility for their own roles, growth and outcomes will occur. Ultimately, the whole point of building greater trust, conflict, commitment, and accountability is one thing: the achievement of results. No matter how good a team feels about itself or its outcomes, if goals are not achieved, then it is not a good team.

Cohesive teams work together to achieve a goal despite conflict and trials. They embrace the need to commit themselves to learn from one another and build the trust that will enable them to cross the finish line together. On the other hand, a non-cohesive team is only concerned with individual members looking good whether the team achieves its goal or not. Being seen as the MVP (most valuable player) of a team is great, but what really matters is winning the game. This is one reason why goals are shared across the entire team—and the only way for a team to maximize its output toward these goals is to establish the same priorities and row in the same direction.

> Cohesive teams work together to achieve a goal despite conflict and trials.

When consulting with a large gym company that had multiple locations, it was discovered that most of the gyms' managers were leading from their own direction and doing their own thing. If an employee went from one gym to another one in the company, they discovered that things were being done in a totally different way. My consulting team decided to visit all seven gyms, posing as customers interested in getting a membership, when we were really covertly analyzing each gym's internal processes. After a detailed study of each location, we brought all the managers together for a "best practices" seminar. The managers were not even aware that there was no continuity in processes and services between gyms. They corrected this, and it resulted in better customer experience and improved revenues.

A God-A-Tude of Teamwork requires everyone to let go of ego and selfish ambition and come together with others to achieve excellence and success. When it comes to our performance, motivational speaker and self-improvement author Brian Tracy talks about having a positive mental attitude, and he believes that approximately 85 percent of our performance is based on our attitude. Positive mental attitude is essential to understanding ourselves in concert with understanding others to obtain maximum outcome.

DAILY DEVOTION TO YOUR GOD-A-TUDE

If you want to lead, if you want to grow, and if you want to be better, it all starts with your mindset. If you want to be rich, you can't have a poverty mentality. If you want to be the head, you can't stay the tail. Your God-A-Tude puts you in another place and carries you to an optimum state of optimism, hard work, and patience.

Therefore, you must intentionally strive each day to have a God-A-Tude that will enable you to achieve anything you want in life and to positively impact the people around you. It is not just going to happen. You must wake up every morning with a mindset that there are no bad days—only good days that will have challenges to overcome—challenges that will make you better and stronger.

Every day, I read something positive, listen to something positive, and try to find something positive in everything I see and do. You have to train your mind every single day. This is not a lifestyle that denies the realities of life or the negatives around you. Rather, it is a daily devotion in which you tool your mind so that when the challenges come (and they will), you will be able to respond in a proactive and productive manner that reflects the different God-A-Tudes I have detailed throughout this book. No matter what is going on or how things appear, when we exercise our God-A-Tude, we will not have bad days.

Join me in pursuing the things of God and life with the proper attitude to succeed.

You'll never be the same.

Made in the USA
Monee, IL
23 December 2021